40-Day Journey with Martin Luther

Other books in the

40-DAY *Journey* Series

40-Day Journey with Joan Chittister
Beverly Lanzetta, Editor

40-Day Journey with Dietrich Bonhoeffer
Ron Klug, Editor

40-Day Journey with Kathleen Norris
Kathryn Haueisen, Editor

40-DAY

Journey

WITH MARTIN LUTHER

40-Day Journey Series

Gracia M. Grindal, Editor

Augsburg Books

Minneapolis

40-DAY JOURNEY WITH MARTIN LUTHER

Copyright © 2008 Augsburg Books, an imprint of Augsburg Fortress. All rights reserved. Except for brief quotations in critical articles or reviews, no part of this book may be reproduced in any manner without prior written permission from the publisher. Visit www.augsburgfortress.org /copyrights/contact.asp or write to Permissions, Augsburg Fortress, Publishers, Box 1209, Minneapolis, MN 55440-1209.

Scripture quotations are from the New Revised Standard Version Bible, copyright © 1989 by the Division of Christian Education of the National Council of the Churches of Christ in the USA. Used by permission. All rights reserved.

Cover image: Detail of Portrait of Martin Luther by Lucas Cranach the Elder, 1533. Germanisches National Museum, Nuremberg, Germany.
Cover design: Laurie Ingram
Book design: PerfecType, Nashville, Tenn.

Library of Congress Cataloging-in-Publication Data
Luther, Martin, 1483-1546.
40-day journey with Martin Luther / Gracia Grindal, editor.
    p. cm. — (40-day journey series)
Includes bibliographical references.
ISBN 978-0-8066-8039-2 (alk. paper)
1. Theology—16th century. 2. Theology—Early works to 1800. 3. Devotional exercises. I. Grindal, Gracia. II. Title. III. Title: Forty day journey with Martin Luther.
BR331.E5G75 2008
230'.41—dc22
          2007042367

The paper used in this publication meets the minimum requirements of American National Standard for Information Sciences—Permanence of Paper for Printed Library Materials, ANSI Z329.48-1984.

CONTENTS

SERIES INTRODUCTION

Imagine spending forty days with a great spiritual guide who has both the wisdom and the experience to help you along the path of your own spiritual journey. Imagine being able to listen to and question spiritual guides from the past and the present. Imagine being, as it were, mentored by women and men who have made their own spiritual journey and have recorded the landmarks, detours, bumps in the road, potholes, and wayside rests that they encountered along the way—all to help others (like you) who must make their own journey.

The various volumes in Augsburg Books' *40-Day Journey Series* are all designed to do just that—to lead you where your mind and heart and spirit long to go. As Augustine once wrote: *"You have made us for yourself, O Lord, and our heart is restless until it rests in you."* The wisdom you will find in the pages of this series of books will give you the spiritual tools and direction to find that rest. But there is nothing quietistic in the spirituality you will find here. Those who would guide you on this journey have learned that the heart that rests in God is one that lives with deeper awareness, deeper creativity, deeper energy, and deeper passion and commitment to the things that matter to God.

An ancient Chinese proverb states the obvious: the journey of a thousand miles begins with the first step. In a deep sense, books in the *40-Day Journey Series* are first steps on a journey that will not end when the forty days are over. No one can take the first step (or any step) for you.

Imagine that you are on the banks of the Colorado River. You are here to go white-water rafting for the first time and your guide has just described the experience, telling you with graphic detail what to expect. It sounds both exciting and frightening. You long for the experience but are somewhat disturbed, anxious, uncertain in the face of the danger that promises to accompany you on the journey down the river. The guide gets into the raft. She will accompany you on the journey, *but she can't take the journey for you.* If you want to experience the wildness of the river, the raw beauty of the canyon, the camaraderie of adventurers, and the mystery of a certain oneness with nature (and nature's creator), then you've got to get in the boat.

This book in your hand is like that. It describes the journey, provides a "raft," and invites you to get in. Along with readings from your spiritual guide, you will find scripture to mediate on, questions to ponder, and suggestions for personal journaling, guidance in prayer, and a prayer for the day. If done faithfully each day, you will find the wisdom and encouragement you need to integrate meaningful spiritual practices into your daily life. And when the 40-day journey is over it no longer will be the guide's description of the journey that stirs your longing for God but *your own experience* of the journey that grounds your faith and life and keeps you on the path.

I would encourage you to pick up other books in the series. There is only one destination, but many ways to get there. Not everything in every book will work for you (we are all unique), but in every book you will find much to help you discover your own path on the journey to the One in whom we all "live and move and have our being" (Acts 17:28).

May all be well with you on the journey.
Henry F. French, Series Editor

PREFACE

Not long after Martin Luther realized that we are saved by faith alone, he also realized that he had to provide devotional resources for his followers consistent with his discovery. As he developed devotional resources for the laity, he understood that the materials needed to be simple and easily grasped by even the youngest child. To that end he based his major devotional resource—the Small Catechism—on the three parts of the Catechism long accepted in Christendom, namely, the Ten Commandments, the Apostles' Creed, and the Lord's Prayer.

Luther noted many times that the Commandments, the Creed, and the Lord's Prayer were so simple anyone could say them, but even he, a learned Doctor of Theology, could not plumb their depths. "For in these three parts everything contained in the Scriptures is comprehended in short, plain, and simple terms." They "summed up the teaching, life, wisdom, and learning that constitute the Christian's conversation, conduct and concern."

Your 40-day journey begins with selections from Luther in which he advises us how and when to pray—advice which should serve as a helpful guide for the rest of the forty days when Luther's Catechism itself is the subject of study.

Take the opportunity to focus intently on the Catechism and Luther's answers. Commit them to memory if you will. Linger on small parts of it throughout the day as it occurs to you. In the text you will find several suggestions from Luther as to how to live a life of prayer. One of the best known is what he called "a garland of prayer." The garland consists of four questions to ask of any biblical text you read: (1) What does it teach? (2) What should I give thanks for? (3) What does it convict me of or cause regret about in my daily life and (4) What will I ask for or petition for. Let these questions, this "garland of prayer," guide you as you meditate on the texts given to you in your *40-Day Journey with Martin Luther*.

One note: as you make your way through this material, you will see clearly that Luther's time was very different from ours. He uses language and metaphors that may seem strange to modern ears and minds. It will take careful and critical thought, but there is a rich reward for those who make the journey. Try to see into his age and use what you can for you own life.

For Luther the Christian life, a pitched battle between Christ and Satan, was to be lived in confidence and serenity because Christ had thwarted sin, death, and the power of the devil. For Luther, Christ is always the victor, the one who went to the depths to win us over. His words should give us the same confidence as we learn to trust more simply and profoundly in Christ.

Gracia Grindal

How to Use this Book

Your 40-day journey with Martin Luther gives you the opportunity to be mentored by one of the great spiritual writers and Christian leaders of the past millennium. The purpose of the journey, however, is not just to gain "head knowledge" about Luther. Rather, it is to begin living what you learn.

You will probably benefit most by fixing a special time of day in which to "meet with" your spiritual mentor. It is easier to maintain a spiritual practice if you do it regularly at the same time. For many people mornings, while the house is still quiet and before the busyness of the day begins, is a good time. Others will find that the noon hour or before bedtime serves well. We are all unique. Some of us are "morning people" and some of us are not. Do whatever works *for you* to maintain a regular meeting with Luther. Write it into your calendar and do your best to keep your appointments.

It is best if you complete your 40-day journey in forty days. A deepening focus and intensity of experience will be the result. However, it is certainly better to complete the journey than to give it up because you can't get it done in forty days. Indeed, making it a 40- or 20-week journey may better fit your schedule and it just might be that spending a whole week or half a week reflecting on the reading, the scripture, and the prayers, and practicing what you are learning could be a powerfully transforming experience as well. Again, set a schedule that works for you, only be consistent.

Most days of the journey begin with a reading from Luther's *Small Catechism*, and his commentary on the topic from the *Large Catechism*. You will note that the readings, from day to day, build on each other and introduce you to key ideas in Luther's understanding of Christian life and faith. Read each selection slowly, letting the words sink into your consciousness. You may want to read each selection two or three times before moving on, perhaps reading it out loud once. Luther recommended that one could spend a lifetime of devotions on the Ten Commandments, the Apostles' Creed, and the

Lord's Prayer. You might want to memorize them, if you haven't already, before you begin to focus on them during your daily time of study and prayer.

Following the reading from Luther, you will find the heading *Biblical Wisdom* and a brief passage from the Bible that relates directly to what Luther has said. As with the selection from Luther, read the biblical text slowly, letting the words sink into your consciousness.

Following the biblical reading, you will find the heading *Silence for Meditation*. Here you should take anywhere from five to twenty minutes meditating on the two readings. Begin by getting centered. Sit with your back straight, eyes closed, hands folded in your lap and breathe slowly and deeply. Remember that breath is a gift of God, it is God's gift of life. Do nothing for two or three minutes other than simply observe your breath. Focus your awareness on the end of your nose. Feel the breath enter through your nostrils and leave through your nostrils.

Once you feel your mind and spirit settling down, open your eyes and read the Luther text and the biblical text again. Read them slowly, focus on each word or phrase, savor them, explore possible meanings and implications. At the end of each day you will find a blank page with the heading *Notes*. As you meditate on the readings, jot down any insights that occur to you. Do the readings raise any questions for you? Write them down. Do the readings suggest anything you should do? Write it down.

Stay at it as long as it feels useful. When your mind is ready to move on, close your eyes and observe your breath for a minute or so. Then return to the book and the next heading—*Questions to Ponder*. Here you will find a few pointed questions on the reading from Luther and the Scripture. These are general questions intended for all Christians and communities of faith. Think them through and write your answers (and the implications of your answers for your own life of faith and for your community of faith) in the *Notes* section.

When you have finished with the *Questions to Ponder*, move on to the *Psalm Fragment*. Luther was a Professor of Old Testament, and he lived passionately in the psalms. He thought of them as the prayers of Jesus that we could also pray with Christ. The *Psalm Fragment* is a brief passage from one of the Psalms that relates to what you have already read. Again, read it slowly and savor the words. It may give you another perspective on the day's readings and help unpack their meaning further.

Following the *Psalm Fragment*, you will find the heading *Journal Reflections*. Several suggestions for journaling are given that apply the readings to your own personal experience. It is in journaling that the "day" reaches its climax and the potential for transformative change is greatest. It would be best to buy a separate journal rather than use the *Notes* section of the book. For a journal you can use a spiral-bound or ring-bound notebook or one of the hardcover journal books sold in stationery stores. Below are some suggestions for how to keep a journal. For now, let's go back to the 40-day journey book.

The *Questions to Ponder* and *Journal Reflections* exercises are meant to assist you in reflecting on the Luther and Scripture quotations. Do not feel that you have to answer every question. You may choose which questions or exercises are most helpful to you. Sometimes a perfectly appropriate response to a question is, "I don't know" or "I'm not sure what I think about that." The important thing is to record your own thoughts and questions.

After *Journal Reflections*, you will find two more headings. The first is *Prayers for the Life of Faith*. Luther recommended that we bring simply everything to God in prayer and these suggestions are merely ideas that bubble up from the readings. Under this heading you will find suggestions for petitionary and intercessory prayer that relate to the key points in the day's readings. The last heading (before *Notes*) is *Prayer for Today*, a one line prayer to end your "appointment" with Luther, and to be prayed from time to time throughout the day.

Hints on Keeping a Journal

A journal is a very helpful tool. Keeping a journal is a form of meditation, a profound way of getting to know yourself—and God—more deeply. Although you could read your 40-day journey book and reflect on it "in your head," writing can help you focus your thoughts, clarify your thinking, and keep a record of your insights, questions, and prayers. Writing is generative: it enables you to have thoughts you would not otherwise have had.

A few hints for journaling

1. Write in your journal with grace. Don't get stuck in trying to do it perfectly. Just write freely. Don't worry about literary style, spelling, or grammar. Your goal is simply to generate thoughts pertinent to your own life and get them down on paper.
2. You may want to begin and end your journaling with prayer. Ask for the guidance and wisdom of the Spirit (and thank God for that guidance and wisdom when you are done).
3. If your journaling takes you in directions that go beyond the journaling questions in your 40-day book, go there. Let the questions encourage, not limit your writing.
4. Respond honestly. Don't write what you think you're supposed to believe. Write down what you really do believe, in so far as you can identify that. If you don't know, or are not sure, or if you have questions, record those. Questions are often openings to spiritual growth.
5. Carry your 40-day book and journal around with you every day during your journey (only keep them safe from prying eyes). The 40-day journey process is an intense experience that doesn't stop when you close the book. Your mind and heart and spirit will be engaged all day, and it will be helpful to have your book and journal handy to take notes or make new entries as they occur to you.

Journeying with Others

You can use your 40-day book with another person—a spiritual friend or partner—or with a small group. It would be best for each person to first do his or her own reading, reflection, and writing in solitude. Then when you come together, share the insights you have gained from your time alone. Your discussion will probably focus on the *Questions to Ponder,* however, if the relationship is intimate, you may feel comfortable sharing some of what you have written in your journal. No one, however, should ever be pressured to share anything in their journal if they are not comfortable doing so.

Remember that your goal is to learn from one another, not to argue, nor to prove that you are right and the other person wrong. Just practice listening and trying to understand why your partner, friend, or colleague thinks as he or she does.

Practicing intercessory prayer together, you will find, will strengthen the spiritual bonds of those who take the journey together. And as you all work to translate insight into action, sharing your experience with each other is a way of encouraging and guiding each other and provides the opportunity to correct each other gently if that becomes necessary.

Continuing the Journey

When the forty days (or forty weeks) is over, a milestone has been reached, but the journey needn't end. One goal of the 40-day series is to introduce you to a particular spiritual guide with the hope that, having whet your appetite, you will want to keep the journey going. At the end of the book are some suggestions for further reading that will take you deeper on your journey with Martin Luther.

WHO WAS MARTIN LUTHER?

Martin Luther (1483-1546) stands at the hinge of the last millennium. As the last years of the twentieth century came to an end, scholars and pundits almost universally agreed that Luther's mind and influence were second to none in the millennium except for Albert Einstein.

When Luther, a young Augustinian monk, pounded his Ninety-five Theses to the door of the Castle Church in Wittenberg, Saxony, in the southeastern part of Germany, he drove a stake into the heart of the medieval world. The medieval church, by almost everyone's estimation, was ripe for reform, and Luther spoke at just the right time. He—as many before him—had watched with growing disgust the corruption of Rome, basically the only Christian church in Europe at the time.

For Luther it came to a head when he observed the selling of indulgences —forgiveness—to people who were genuinely terrorized by the thought of ending up in the clutches of Satan in Hell, a fate vividly portrayed in the iconography of the time. When he had his legendary flash of insight, the story has it that he was reading Romans 5:1: "Therefore being justified by faith, we have peace with God through our Lord Jesus Christ." Everything changed. *He was not to make peace with God; God made peace with him through Jesus Christ.* Faith was a gift given to him by a gracious God who, at the cost of his only son, had won eternal salvation for him and snatched him from the hands of sin, death, and the power of the devil. At last, Luther had found peace.

In many ways Luther's reform of the church began as a devotional or spiritual crisis. As a young monk, Luther suffered terrors that came from his spiritual "scrupulosity." He was tormented by the impossibility of keeping the First Commandment—to love God above all things. He had entered monastic life to please God and find peace. Becoming a monk, however, made the problem worse. Following the remedies of the spiritual disciplines recommended by the church—more devotion, more fasting, more praying, more self-denial—simply drove him further into despair. The more he knew about God, the more he knew he could not measure up. God became a torment to him. After his discovery he found peace and began to work his insight into the gospel through everything he did from then on.

His nailing of the Theses to the door shook Christendom to its foundation. Europe, ruled by a combination of princes and bishops who had both spiritual and temporal powers, was ready for reform. At the same time, the powers that be viewed any threat to their hegemony with alarm. One could expect a brutal response from the civil and religious authorities if one attacked them as Luther did. After his Ninety-five Theses became well known, the church and empire watched Luther closely for any signs of heresy or insubordination.

The crisis came to a head in Leipzig during June of 1519, when Luther debated with John Eck. At issue was whether or not the church was over Scripture. Luther argued that popes and councils can err; Christ did not. This direct attack on the power of the church and papacy could not be overlooked by Rome. Not long after the debate, Luther was threatened with excommunication if he did not recant. In the meantime, he continued writing some of his most provocative treatises, most enflaming among them his *Address to the Christian Nobility*, in which he argued for the priesthood of all believers, a direct attack on the power of the clergy. Not long after that, he produced his *Babylonian Captivity of the Church*, which attacked the Roman sacramental system point by point, and finally, *The Freedom of a Christian*.

Each of these writings brought him closer to excommunication; at the same time, however, they were greeted with astonishment by many who agreed with him. All without exception caused great offense to both Rome and the Emperor. His prince, Duke Friedrich the Wise, proud of this exciting theologian at his new university in little Wittenberg, protected Luther from the increasing threats of the Holy Roman Emperor, Charles V, and the Pope.

At the Diet of Worms in 1521, Luther was formally asked to recant his writings, which he most spectacularly refused to do with the famous words, "Here I stand. I can do no other. God help me. Amen." With that he was declared an outlaw in Europe and could not be guaranteed safe-conduct anywhere. Luther's life was in danger. On his way home from Worms, Luther's prince had him "kidnapped" and brought to the Wartburg Castle. There he stayed for some months disguised as Junker George.

While hidden away, Luther began to translate the Bible into a rich idiomatic German, which shaped the German language much as the King James Version of the Bible (1611) did for English. When violence broke out in Wittenberg over the reforms begun by Luther's followers, Luther could not remain hidden any longer and returned to his home in the Black Cloister in

Wittenberg. Although in great danger, he lived in Wittenberg for the rest of his life, protected by his prince.

His production of treatises, translations, and devotional reforms continued apace even while he was under great duress. After the translation of the Bible, he turned his attention to other resources for the education and edification of the laity, always informed by his theological discovery that faith was a gift kindled by the word of God. In the area of prayer and worship, the most important thing was to hear the word of God first, not to perform deeds of spiritual virtuosity that we imagined would please God. By 1523 he had prepared a German language version of the Holy Communion service, as well as several hymns in German that the people began to sing lustily in their services—for now they had the gospel in their own language. These hymns not only taught the new evangelical faith, they helped the laity to preach God's word to one another, something we hear most clearly in his greatest hymn, *A Mighty Fortress Is Our God*, a sermon on Psalm 46, with images of medieval Germany, not ancient Israel.

By 1526 he had prepared a new version of the Communion Service (the German Mass), this time with German hymns and liturgy to be sung in place of Latin. During this time, he also was embroiled in a theological debate on free will with the great humanist Desiderius Erasmus. Luther's response was the magisterial *Bondage of the Will*.

In the civil realm he had to deal with the horrifying outbreak of the Peasant's War, in which the peasants took his ideas to mean something he had not intended. His reaction against the peasants and their leader, Thomas Münzer, encouraging the prince to violently put them down, seems brutal and shocking to us today, but it was consistent with the times.

During these very same years, in June of 1525, he surprised himself by marrying Katherine von Bora, a run-away nun. Together they founded the Protestant parsonage, establishing its traditions of hospitality and mercy to the needy in the community. Martin and Katie modeled the Christian family as they raised and taught their children the faith.

By the end of the decade, Luther, now the theological leader of a new church known in Europe as the Evangelical Church, (Americans call it Lutheran) was appalled to discover, in visitations to the congregations in Saxony, that the people knew very little about their Christian faith, nor were their poor and ill-educated pastors able to teach it very well.

Good God, what wretchedness I beheld! The common people, especially those who live in the country, have no knowledge whatsoever of Christian teaching, and unfortunately many pastors are quite incompetent and unfitted for teaching. Although the people are supposed to be Christians, are baptized, and receive the holy sacrament, they do not know the Lord's Prayer, the Creed, or Ten Commandments, they live as if they were pigs and irrational beasts, and now that the gospel has been restored, they have mastered the fine art of abusing liberty.

To remedy this situation he began preaching regular sermons on the basics of the Christian faith in the city church in Wittenberg. These resulted in his classic *Small Catechism*, which came out in May, 1529, followed by his *Large Catechism*. This, his most productive decade, concluded fittingly with these resources for people who needed to be taught the Christian faith so they could practice it in their homes, work, and congregations. Until his death, he thought the *Small Catechism* to be among his best work.

It is well to remember that this most brilliant of scholars did his best work when he saw how a theological idea affected the spiritual lives of his people. He did not think it beneath him to devote himself to the teaching of children and the laity, and he provided parents with resources so they could teach their children in the home. Thus, his *Small Catechism*, which is the basis of this *40-Day Journey with Martin Luther*, became the backbone of the Lutheran movement in Europe. After the *Small Catechism* became part of the life of the early Lutherans, when pastors and church leaders would try to abandon its simple teachings, the people would rise up against them with the words of their dear Dr. Luther.

When Luther died in 1546, Europe and Christendom were changed utterly. Luther had been the crucial voice at the crucial time. His passionate conviction that faith and salvation came from Christ alone, his protean theological imagination, and phenomenal productivity quickly spread his ideas throughout Europe.

His capacity to change and grow in his own life gave him what became a happy and joyful marriage—he would very soon be calling his wife, the gifted and strong Katherine von Bora, Herr Katie, and the stories of the marriage between these two strong-willed people continued to amuse and amaze people who might not have predicted much success for such a marriage.

While in his youth his spirituality had advised strongly against marriage and the dangers of women, he was able to change those opinions for himself and his followers when he began to see the joy there was in family and children. This had a remarkable effect on western spirituality, which since Augustine had devalued the carnal world.

Although violence, war, famine, and terror followed in the wake of the Reformation, Luther's voice still speaks loudly and clearly to Christians throughout the world as they struggle to understand who God is, what God did for us in Christ Jesus, and the blessings and complications of our vocation in this world devoted to the work of God as we serve the neighbor. While he was no saint, and history is replete with the records of his failures (most lamentably his statements on the Jews), he is the theologian most theologians concede understood God the best. His attack on the corruption of the church, his holding up of the rights and responsibilities of the laity to practice their vocations as holy callings blessed by God, his recommendation that both boys and girls learn to read and write so they could study the Scriptures, still resonate throughout secular, liberal democracies around the world. His voice, though now not so well known, is still working its way through our daily lives as we struggle to be Christians in a rich, complicated, and troubling world.

May your *40-Day Journey with Martin Luther* deepen and enrich your life of faith.

40-DAY
Journey

WITH MARTIN LUTHER

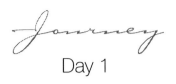

Day 1

I WILL TELL YOU AS best I can what I do personally when I pray. May our dear Lord grant to you and to everybody to do it better than I! Amen.

First, when I feel that I have become cool and joyless in prayer because of other tasks or thought (for the flesh and the devil always impede and obstruct prayer), I take my little Psalter, hurry to my room, or, if it be the day and hour for it, to the church where a congregation is assembled and, as time permits, I say quietly to myself and word-for-word the Ten Commandments, the Creed, and, if I have time, some words of Christ or of Paul, or some psalms, just as a child might do.

BIBLICAL WISDOM

Take the helmet of salvation, and the sword of the Spirit, which is the word of God. Pray in the Spirit at all times in every prayer and supplication. To that end keep alert and always persevere in supplication for all the saints. Ephesians 6:17

SILENCE FOR MEDITATION

QUESTIONS TO PONDER

- What is Luther's solution for coolness and joylessness in prayer? Does it seem a good solution? Why or why not?
- How do you, your faith community, and your culture think about the "devil?"
- Why does the "devil" want to impede us in our prayer? What obstructions to prayer have you experienced?

Psalm Fragment

Come, bless the LORD, all you servants of the LORD,
who stand by night in the house of the LORD!
Lift up your hands to the holy place,
and bless the LORD.
May the LORD, maker of heaven and earth,
bless you from Zion. Psalm 134:1-3

Journal Reflections

- Describe in your journal your own present practice of prayer.
- Write the Ten Commandments, the Apostles' Creed, and the Lord's Prayer, in your journal. If you haven't already done it, memorize them.
- Write down what you want to learn about the life of faith as you begin these forty days.

Prayers for the Life of Faith

Pray that God will give you (and any others who join you in this journey) joy in these next forty days as you study the Commandments, Creed, and Lord's Prayer.

Prayer for Today

Lord Jesus, thank you for your great disciple Martin Luther. Help me learn how to dwell in your word always.

Notes

IT IS A GOOD THING to let prayer be the first business of the morning and the last at night. Guard yourself carefully against those false, deluding ideas which tell you, "Wait a little while. I will pray in an hour; first I must attend to this or that." Such thoughts get you away from prayer into other affairs which so hold your attention and involve you that nothing comes of prayer for that day... When your heart has been warmed by such recitation to yourself [of the Ten Commandments, the words of Christ, etc.] and is intent upon the matter, kneel or stand with your hands folded and your eyes toward heaven and speak or think as briefly as you can:

> O Heavenly Father, dear God, I am a poor unworthy sinner. I do not deserve to raise my eyes or hands toward thee or to pray. But because thou has commanded us all to pray and hast promised to hear us and through thy dear Son Jesus Christ hast taught us both how and what to pray, I come to thee in obedience to thy word, trusting in thy gracious promise. I pray in the name of my Lord Jesus Christ together with all thy saints and Christians on earth as he has taught us: "Our Father who art"...through the whole prayer, word for word.

BIBLICAL WISDOM

And we urge you, beloved, to admonish the idlers, encourage the faint hearted, help the weak, be patient with all of them. See that none of you repays evil for evil, but always seek to do good to one another and to all. Rejoice always, pray without ceasing, give thanks in all circumstances; for this is the will of God in Christ Jesus for you. I Thessalonians 5:14-18

SILENCE FOR MEDITATION

QUESTIONS TO PONDER

- Why (and how) is the heart warmed by the recitation of the Ten Commandments and the words of Christ? Does your faith community encourage such recitation? If so, in what ways? If not, why not?
- Why do you think Luther recommends a certain position of the body as important for the beginning of prayer?
- How is it possible to "pray without ceasing"?

PSALM FRAGMENT

Give ear to my words, O LORD;
give heed to my sighing.
Listen to the sound of my cry,
my King and my God,
for to you I pray.
O LORD, in the morning you hear my voice;
in the morning I plead my case to you, and watch. Psalm 5:1-3

JOURNAL REFLECTIONS

- Reflect on any difficulties you may have had in the past in keeping a regular schedule of prayer. See whether or not you can detect "false, deluding ideas" that have kept you from keeping a schedule.
- Meditate on the expression "pray without ceasing." To what degree does it define your experience? Think back to yesterday and write down the several times (and ways in which) you may have called upon God.
- Reflect on how it makes you feel to know that the saints in heaven and on earth are praying with you (and you are praying with them).

PRAYERS FOR THE LIFE OF FAITH

Pray that you (and anyone journeying with you) can establish and keep a schedule of prayer faithfully through the next forty days.

PRAYER FOR TODAY

Dear Lord Jesus, I thank you that you have given me the words with which to pray. Thank you that I can come to you any time in prayer with any concern at all.

NOTES

Day 3

I DO NOT BIND MYSELF to such words or syllables, but say my prayers in one fashion today, in another tomorrow, depending upon my mood and feeling. I stay however, as nearly as I can, with the same general thoughts and ideas. It may happen occasionally that I may get lost among so many ideas in one petition (of the Lord's prayer) that I forego the other six. If such an abundance of good thoughts comes to us we ought to disregard the other petitions, make room for such thoughts, listen in silence, and under no circumstances obstruct them. The Holy Spirit himself preaches here, and one word of his sermon is far better than a thousand of our prayers.

BIBLICAL WISDOM

Day by day, as they spent much time together in the temple, they broke bread at home and ate their food with glad and generous hearts, praising God and having the goodwill of all the people. And day by day the Lord added to their number those who were being saved. Acts 2:46-47

SILENCE FOR MEDITATION

QUESTIONS TO PONDER

- What is the difference between "an abundance of good thoughts" and just thinking of too many things at once? How can you tell the difference when you pray, and what might you do if you find yourself thinking too many things at once?
- Luther believed that when we focus on God's word, the Holy Spirit speaks to us in the "abundance of good thoughts" that come to us. Why does Luther insist that hearing what the Holy Spirit has to say is more important than our prayers?
- How much of prayer is listening? How do you listen in prayer? How do you know you are hearing God and not yourself?

Psalm Fragment

On the day I called, you answered me,
you increased my strength of soul. Psalm 138:3

Journal Reflections

- Remember times when you have been praying and your mind has suddenly been filled with good thoughts. Were they from the Holy Spirit or your own distractions? How do you know?
- Reflect on times when you have simply been silent during your devotions. What comes to you? Describe one such time in detail.
- Do you experience "singleness of heart" in your life of faith and in your prayer? If so, describe the experience. If not, how might you achieve it?

Prayers for the Life of Faith

Pray that you will be given the ability to concentrate in your prayers so you can hear God's word (and the Spirit) more clearly and fully.

Prayer for Today

Holy Spirit, enliven this time of prayer for me. Teach me to know when you are speaking and to listen to what you have to say.

Notes

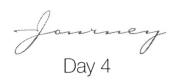

Day 4

IF I HAVE HAD TIME and opportunity to go through the Lord's Prayer, I do the same with the Ten Commandments. I take one part after another and free myself as much as possible from distractions in order to pray. I divide each commandment into four parts, thereby fashioning a garland of four strands. That is, I think of each commandment as, first, instruction, which is really what it is intended to be, and consider what the Lord God demands of me so earnestly. Second, I turn it into a thanksgiving; third, a confession; and fourth, a prayer.

BIBLICAL WISDOM

Do not let loyalty and faithfulness forsake you; bind them around your neck, write them on the tablet of your heart. So you will find favor and good repute in the sight of God and of people. Trust in the LORD with all your heart, and do not rely on your own insight. In all your ways acknowledge him, and he will make straight your paths. Proverbs 3:3-6

SILENCE FOR MEDITATION

QUESTIONS TO PONDER

- Note the order of the four strands in the garland of prayer that Luther recommends. Why do you think they come in that order?
- Why do you think Luther understands the garland of prayer as a response to the word of God?
- How might your community of faith use the garland of prayer in public worship?

Psalm Fragment

You who live in the shelter of the Most High,
*   who abide in the shadow of the Almighty,*
*   will say to the LORD, "My refuge and my fortress;*
*   my God, in whom I trust." Psalm 91:1-4*

Journal Reflections

- Reflect on your own method of meditating on Scripture. Have you ever used Luther's method? If so, describe its effect on you. If not, why not try it?
- Write about how you might begin to make the garland of prayer a regular habit in your faith life.
- Practice this garland of prayer using the *Psalm Fragment*.

Prayers for the Life of Faith

Pray that you will learn to follow the garland of prayer method in both your reading of Scripture and your response in prayer to what you read.

Prayer for Today

Gracious God, open my mind and heart to your word as I mine your word for its depths and riches.

Notes

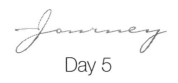

Day 5

WHERE THERE IS TO BE true prayer, there must be utter earnestness. We must feel our need, the distress that drives and impels us to cry out. Then prayer will come spontaneously, as it should, and no one will need to be taught how to prepare for it or how to create the proper devotion… God…wants you to lament and express your needs and concerns, not because he is unaware of them, but in order that you may kindle your heart to stronger and greater desires and open and spread your apron wide to receive many things.

BIBLICAL WISDOM

But whenever you pray, go into your room and shut the door and pray to your Father who is in secret; and your Father who sees in secret will reward you.
Matthew 6:6

SILENCE FOR MEDITATION

QUESTIONS TO PONDER

- Why does Luther say that it is only with earnestness and distress that "prayer will come spontaneously"?
- Luther suggests that our prayers do more for us than for God. How does prayer intensify our relationship with God?
- What does it mean that prayer kindles in us "stronger and greater desires" and causes us to "spread our apron wide to receive"?

PSALM FRAGMENT

With my whole heart I cry; answer me, O LORD.
I will keep your statutes.
I cry to you; save me,
    that I may observe your decrees.

I rise before dawn and cry for help;
I put my hope in your words.
My eyes are awake before each watch of the night,
that I may meditate on your promise. Psalm 119:145-48

JOURNAL REFLECTIONS

- For Luther prayer is really quite simple, it is about our being driven by our earnestness and distress to pray to God. In your journal, reflect on whether or not this is true. When do you feel closest to God?
- The Psalmist cries out with his whole heart. Describe a time when your "whole heart" was at prayer. What feelings were evoked in you?
- Jesus suggests that prayer is best when it is done in secret. What does it mean to you that God is "in secret"? Do you have a "secret" place, a quiet place, a sacred place of your own for prayer? If so, describe it. If not, perhaps you should find one.

PRAYERS FOR THE LIFE OF FAITH

Pray that you will grow in your understanding of prayer and in your relationship with the Lord and that those dearest to you will open up their "whole" hearts to the Lord in prayer so that together you can come to know the Lord's love and grow to live more fully in him.

PRAYER FOR TODAY

Dear Lord Jesus, I pray to you in the confidence that you hear my prayer, and I trust your promise that when I pray you will hear my cry.

NOTES

Journey

Day 6

YOU ARE TO HAVE NO other Gods.

What is this?

Answer: We are to fear, love, and trust God above all things.

A "god" is the term for that to which we are to look for all good and in which we are to find refuge in all need. Therefore, to have a god is nothing else than to trust and believe in that one with your whole heart. As I have often said, it is the trust and faith of the heart alone that make both God and an idol. If your faith and trust are right, then your God is the true one. Conversely, where your trust is false and wrong, there you do not have the true God. For these two belong together, faith and God. Anything on which your heart relies and depends, I say, that is really your God.

BIBLICAL WISDOM

Then God spoke all these words: I am the Lord your God, who brought you out of the land of Egypt, out of the house of slavery; you shall have no other gods before me. You shall not make for yourself an idol, whether in the form of anything that is in heaven above, or that is on the earth beneath, or that is in the water under the earth. You shall not bow down to them or worship them; for I the Lord your God am a jealous God… Exodus 20:1-5a

SILENCE FOR MEDITATION

QUESTIONS TO PONDER

- How is it possible that our faith and trust can "make both God and an idol"?
- What are some of the things (idols) our culture encourages us to place our faith and trust in?
- We are instructed to both "fear" and "love" God. In practical terms, what do you think it means to fear God? To love God?

Psalm Fragment

Their idols are silver and gold,
*   the work of human hands.*
They have mouths, but do not speak;
*   eyes, but do not see.*
They have ears, but do not hear;
*   noses, but do not smell.*
They have hands, but do not feel;
*   feet, but do not walk;*
*   they make no sound in their throats.*
Those who make them are like them;
*   so are all who trust in them.* Psalm 115:4-8

Journal Reflections

- God wants to be in relationship with us. Describe in your journal how you experience your relationship with God at this time.
- Write about how the fear and love of God work themselves out in your daily life.
- It has been said that "the human heart is a factory of idols." In your journal, describe any idols that have been manufactured in your own heart's factory. What kind of "worship" do they demand of you? What would you need to do to be free of these idols?

Prayers for the Life of Faith

Pray for yourself, your family, and your friends that they will put their faith wholly in the one true God and put away all their idols.

Prayer for Today

Lord, cast out those idols in my heart that captivate me and draw me from you. Give me the faith to put all my trust in you alone. Amen.

Notes

Journey

Day 7

YOU ARE NOT TO MISUSE the name of your God.

What is this?

Answer: We are to fear and love God, so that we do not curse, swear, practice magic, lie, or deceive using God's name, but instead use that very name in every time of need to call on, pray to, praise, and give thanks to God.

With the words, "You are not to take the name of God in vain," God at the same time gives us to understand that we are to use his name properly, for it has been revealed and given to us precisely for our use and benefit. Therefore, since we are forbidden here to use his holy name in support of falsehood and wickedness, it follows, conversely, that we are commanded to use it in the service of truth and of all that is good—for example, when we swear properly where it is necessary and required, or also when we teach properly, or again, when we call on God's name in time of need, or thank and praise him in time of prosperity, etc.

BIBLICAL WISDOM

You shall not make wrongful use of the name of the LORD your God, for the LORD will not acquit anyone who misuses his name. Exodus 20:7

SILENCE FOR MEDITATION

QUESTIONS TO PONDER

- Read Exodus 3:13-15. What is God's answer to Moses at the burning bush when asked to give his name? What kind of name is that?
- In what ways does your community of faith use God's name "in the service of truth and of all that is good"?
- How might a community of faith actually "misuse" God's name?

Psalm Fragment

Let them praise the name of the Lord,
for his name alone is exalted;
his glory is above earth and heaven.
He has raised up a horn for his people,
praise for all his faithful,
for the people of Israel who are close to him.
Praise the Lord! Psalm 148:13-14

Journal Reflections

- Meditate on the proper use and misuse of God's name. Make a list in your journal of the ways you properly use God's name. Make another list of the ways you misuse God's name.
- Write a statement in your journal indicating your commitment to increase the proper uses of God's name and to decrease the misuse of God's name in your words and actions.
- We use God's name properly when we "call on God's name in time of need, or thank and praise him" when things are going well for us. Are asking, thanking, and praising God daily "spiritual habits" for you? If so, describe your experience with them. If not, why not work them into your life?

Prayers for the Life of Faith

Call upon the Lord to help you use his name properly so that those who hear and see you may come to know God better.

Prayer for Today

Lord Jesus, teach me the holiness of your name so that when I call to you it is always to ask for help or to thank and praise you and never to curse.

Notes

Journey

Day 8

YOU ARE TO HALLOW THE day of rest.

What is this?

Answer: We are to fear and love God, so that we do not despise preaching or God's Word, but instead keep that Word holy and gladly hear and learn it.

What is meant by "keeping it holy"? Nothing else than devoting it to holy words, holy works, and holy living. The day itself does not need to be made holy, for it was created holy. But God wants it to be holy for you. So it becomes holy or unholy on your account, depending on whether you spend it doing something holy or unholy. How does such sanctifying take place? Not when we sit behind the stove and refrain from hard work, or place a garland on our head and dress up in our best clothes, but... when we make use of God's Word and exercise ourselves in it.

~

BIBLICAL WISDOM

Then he said to them, "The sabbath was made for humankind, and not humankind for the sabbath; so the Son of Man is lord even of the sabbath."
Mark 2:27-28

SILENCE FOR MEDITATION

QUESTIONS TO PONDER

- Luther states that the sabbath should be devoted to "holy words, holy works, and holy living." What does that suggest to you about how we should spend Sunday?
- In what ways is sabbath-keeping countercultural?
- What does it mean to "exercise ourselves in God's word"? How does your community of faith encourage and support such "exercise"?

Psalm Fragment

How lovely is your dwelling place,
*   O Lord of hosts!*
My soul longs, indeed it faints
*   for the courts of the Lord;*
*   my heart and my flesh sing for joy*
*   to the living God...*
Happy are those who live in your house,
*   ever singing your praise.* Psalm 84:1-2, 4

Journal Reflections

- Reflect on the Sundays of your childhood. Write about your favorite memories. Did your family observe the sabbath? How? What did it mean to you? What does it mean to you now?
- Sabbath, or rest, is important to the rhythm of our lives. Is there anything you might do to give your life a better balance between work and rest? Between secular pursuits and holy pursuits?
- Have you ever "longed for the courts of the Lord"? If so, write about the feeling of longing. If not, can you imagine such longing?

Prayers for the Life of Faith

Pray that you and your family will take the time to hear God's word and keep it. Pray for someone you know who needs both rest and the refreshment that comes from hearing God's word.

Prayer for Today

Lord Jesus, you made the sabbath for me to rest in you. May the day become holy for me through the use and exercise of your word.

Notes

Journey

Day 9

YOU ARE TO HONOR YOUR father and your mother.

What is this?

Answer: We are to fear and love God, so that we neither despise nor anger our parents and others in authority, but instead honor, serve, obey, love, and respect them.

First, then, learn what this commandment requires concerning honor to parents. You are to esteem them above all things and to value them as the most precious treasure on earth. Second, in your words you are also to behave respectfully toward them and are not to speak discourteously to them, to criticize them, or to take them to task, but rather to submit to them and hold your tongue, even if they go too far. Third, you are also to honor them by your actions, that is, with your body and possessions, serving them, helping them, and caring for them when they are old, sick, feeble, or poor; all this you should do not only cheerfully, but also with humility and reverence, doing it as if for God.

BIBLICAL WISDOM

"Honor your father and mother"—this is the first commandment with a promise: "so that it may be well with you and you may live long on the earth." And, fathers, do not provoke your children to anger, but bring them up in the discipline and instruction of the Lord. Ephesians 6:2-4

SILENCE FOR MEDITATION

QUESTIONS TO PONDER

- To whom is this commandment addressed—very young children or older children with feeble parents who need their help?
- Luther extends the commandment to honor your father and mother to "others in authority." Who are those others? Does it make sense to bring them under this commandment?

- In what ways does your faith community encourage and support people in keeping this commandment? What more might be done?

Psalm Fragment

The Lord is my chosen portion and my cup;
*   you hold my lot.*
The boundary lines have fallen for me in pleasant places;
*   I have a goodly heritage.* Psalm 16:5-6

Journal Reflections

- Meditate on how the commandment to honor your parents might become a spiritual practice for you.
- Reflect on what you have done or are doing for your parents to honor and help them. Were (or are) these duties burdensome to you or a pleasure for you? Explain.
- What "others in authority" in your life would you bring under the umbrella of this commandment? Why?

Prayers for the Life of Faith

If your parents are still living, pray for strength to continue to honor them. Whether living or dead, give thanks for whatever good they provided you, and pray for the power to forgive them for whatever wrongs they may have done you.

Prayer for Today

Dear Heavenly Father, thank you for being faithful to me, even if I have not honored either you or my parents as I should. Help me to give honor to you and them, and show me how to care for the young who need my help.

Notes

Journey

Day 10

YOU ARE NOT TO KILL.

What is this?

Answer: We are to fear and love God, so that we neither endanger nor harm the lives of our neighbors, but instead help and support them in all of life's needs.

This commandment is violated not only when we do evil, but also when we have the opportunity to do good to our neighbors and to prevent, protect, and save them from suffering bodily harm or injury, but fail to do so. If you send a naked person away when you could clothe him, you have let him freeze to death. If you see anyone who is suffering from hunger and do not feed her, you have let her starve. Likewise, if you see anyone who is innocently condemned or in similar peril and do not save him although you have means and ways to do so, you have killed him. It will be of no help for you to use the excuse that you did not assist their deaths by word or deed, for you have withheld your love from them and robbed them of the kindness by means of which their lives might have been saved.

BIBLICAL WISDOM

Owe no one anything, except to love one another; for the one who loves another has fulfilled the law. The commandments, "You shall not commit adultery; You shall not murder; You shall not steal; You shall not covet"; and any other commandment, are summed up in this word, "Love your neighbor as yourself." Love does no wrong to a neighbor; therefore, love is the fulfilling of the law.
Romans 13:8-11

SILENCE FOR MEDITATION

Questions to Ponder

- How does it change our understanding of this commandment to think of both what we should not do and what we should do?
- What good might it do for us—and our society—if you and I love our enemies and help them to flourish?
- In a world where so much violence is both encouraged and sanctioned by certain "religious groups," how might you both encourage and support the positive understanding of this commandment?

Psalm Fragment

How very good and pleasant it is
*   when kindred live together in unity!*
For there the LORD ordained his blessing,
*   life forevermore.* Psalm 133:1, 3b

Journal Reflections

- Reflect on how you keep this commandment—do you hear only its negative side (do no harm), or does its positive side (do good) cause you to think of your neighbor and his or her needs differently?
- Remember times when you have withheld love from a neighbor or family member and journal about your reasons. What did it feel like? What, if any, consequences were there? Would you do it differently now?
- Are there any friends or family members with whom you are in conflict and you long to be reconciled with? If so, write about steps you can take to begin the process. Take those steps.

Prayers for the Life of Faith

Pray that you may see the world and the people in it with more tenderness.

Prayer for Today

Dear Lord Jesus, help me to keep hatred and contention from my heart and mind, and help me to work for the best for my neighbor.

Notes

Journey

Day 11

YOU ARE NOT TO COMMIT adultery

What is this?

Answer: We are to fear and love God, so that we lead pure and decent lives in word and deed, and each of us loves and honors his or her spouse.

Inasmuch as there is such a shameless mess and cesspool of all sorts of immorality and indecency among us, this commandment is also directed against every form of unchastity, no matter what it is called. Not only is the outward act forbidden, but also every kind of cause, provocation, and means, so that your heart, your lips, and your entire body may be chaste and afford no occasion, aid, or encouragement to unchastity. Not only that, but you are to defend, protect, and rescue your neighbors whenever they are in danger or need, and moreover, even aid and assist them so that they may retain their honor… In short, all are required both to live chastely themselves and also to help their neighbors to do the same.

BIBLICAL WISDOM

You have heard that it was said, "You shall not commit adultery." But I say to you that everyone who looks at a woman with lust has already committed adultery with her in his heart. Matthew 5:27-28

SILENCE FOR MEDITATION

QUESTIONS TO PONDER

- Both Jesus and Luther draw the line on unchastity much more severely than most people. What wisdom do you find in that?
- What are the forms of unchastity that our culture either tolerates or promotes?
- In our highly—if not over—sexualized culture, how can Christians help each other to keep this commandment?

Psalm Fragment

Have mercy on me, O God,
according to your steadfast love;
according to your abundant mercy
blot out my transgressions.
Wash me thoroughly from my iniquity,
and cleanse me from my sin. Psalm 51:1-2

Journal Reflections

- Write in your journal concerning your feelings about the sexual attitudes and pressures of our culture. In what ways does your faith influence your perspective on sex and sexuality?
- Do you know anyone who is struggling with issues of unchastity or adultery? If so, how might you help them in their struggle? If not, can you imagine what steps you might take to help someone in such a struggle?
- Reflect in writing on how your faith and faith community are (or could be) resources for you in maintaining healthy relationships.

Prayers for the Life of Faith

Pray that someone in a troubled marriage or relationship will find the strength to do the right thing. Pray that you will be able to help them.

Prayer for Today

Dear Lord Jesus, keep me pure and chaste today. May my thoughts, language, and action be honorable and always wholesome and upright.

Notes

Journey

Day 12

YOU ARE NOT TO STEAL.

What is this?

Answer: We are to fear and love God, so that we neither take our neighbors' money or property nor acquire them by using shoddy merchandise or crooked deals, but instead help them to improve and protect their property and income.

We are forbidden to do our neighbors any injury or wrong in any way imaginable, whether by damaging, withholding, or interfering with their possessions and property. We are not even to consent to or permit such a thing but are rather to avert and prevent it. In addition, we are commanded to promote and further our neighbors' interests, and when they suffer any want, we are to help, share, and lend to both friends and foes. Anyone who seeks and desires good works will find here more than enough things to do that are heartily acceptable and pleasing to God.

BIBLICAL WISDOM

Do not store up for yourselves treasures on earth, where moth and rust consume and where thieves break in and steal; but store up for yourselves treasures in heaven, where neither moth nor rust consumes and where thieves do not break in and steal. For where your treasure is, there your heart will be also. Matthew 6:19-21

SILENCE FOR MEDITATION

QUESTIONS TO PONDER

- What is the relationship between the commandment not to steal and a Christian's attitude toward possessions? Toward poverty?
- According to Luther, how are we to consider our neighbors' property, and how are we to use our own wealth and possessions with respect to the neighbor? How would the world change if Christians followed Luther's advice?

- How can a faith community help people to have a healthy relationship with money and possessions.

Psalm Fragment

Put no confidence in extortion,
and set no vain hopes on robbery;
if riches increase, do not set your heart on them. Psalm 62:10

Journal Reflections

- Write about how your attitude toward money and possessions influences (and is influenced by) your spiritual life.
- How does your attitude toward money and possessions influence your relationships with others?
- Reflect on both your earthly and heavenly treasures. Write about how well you balance your life between the material and the spiritual.

Prayers for the Life of Faith

Pray that you will balance your own life and your use of what you own so that you will be able to help others with what you have.

Prayer for Today

Lord Jesus, teach me to use what you have given me wisely; give me a good sense for what is best both for my neighbor and my own life.

Notes

Journey

Day 13

YOU ARE NOT TO BEAR false witness against you neighbor.

What is this?

Answer: We are to fear and love God, so that we do not tell lies about our neighbors, betray or slander them, or destroy their reputations. Instead we are to come to their defense, speak well of them, and interpret everything they do in the best possible light.

God wants to hold in check whatever is done with the tongue against a neighbor. This applies to false preachers with their blasphemous teaching, to false judges and witnesses with their rulings in court and their lying and malicious talk outside of court. It applies especially to the detestable, shameless vice of backbiting or slander by which the devil rides us. Of this much could be said. It is a common, pernicious plague that everyone would rather hear evil than good about their neighbors. Even though we ourselves are evil, we cannot tolerate it when anyone speaks evil of us; instead we want to hear the whole world say golden things of us. Yet we cannot bear it when someone says the best things about others.

BIBLICAL WISDOM

For every species of beast and bird, of reptile and sea creature, can be tamed and has been tamed by the human species, but no one can tame the tongue—a restless evil, full of deadly poison. With it we bless the Lord and Father, and with it we curse those who are made in the likeness of God. From the same mouth come blessing and cursing. My brothers and sisters, this ought not to be so. James 3:7-10

SILENCE FOR MEDITATION

QUESTIONS TO PONDER

- Why is the damage the tongue can do so destructive to human society?
- What is there about us that delights in gossip, yet at the same time, we cannot bear to be gossiped about?
- What resources might faith and the community of faith bring to bear in the struggle against "the tongue" and its capacity for evil?

PSALM FRAGMENT

Why do you boast, O mighty one,
of mischief done against the godly?
All day long you are plotting destruction.
Your tongue is like a sharp razor,
you worker of treachery.
You love evil more than good,
and lying more than speaking the truth.
You love all words that devour,
O deceitful tongue. Psalm 52:1-4

JOURNAL REFLECTIONS

- Reflect on a time when you felt betrayed by the false, careless, or malicious speech of another. How did you feel? What did you do? What role did faith play in your response?
- Do you have difficulties taming your tongue? Reflect on times you may have hurt someone by false, careless, or malicious words. How did it make you feel? What might you do to repair the harm done?
- Write down some specific steps you will take to "tame" your tongue.

PRAYERS FOR THE LIFE OF FAITH

Pray for those in your own life whose untamed tongue has hurt others that they may learn to be silent when speaking is hurtful and does no good.

PRAYER FOR TODAY

Dear Lord, keep me quiet and careful in my speech so that I only speak well of my neighbors and friends and work to uphold their reputations.

NOTES

Journey

Day 14

YOU ARE NOT TO COVET your neighbor's house.

What is this?

Answer: We are to fear and love God, so that we do not try to trick our neighbors out of their inheritance or property or try to get it for ourselves by claiming to have a legal right to it and the like, but instead be of help and service to them in keeping what is theirs.

You are not to covet your neighbor's wife, male or female servant, cattle, or whatever is his.

What is this? Answer:

We are to fear and love God, so that we do not entice, force, or steal away from our neighbors their spouses, household workers, or livestock, but instead urge them to stay and fulfill their responsibilities to our neighbors.

These commandments are aimed directly against envy and miserable covetousness, so that God may remove the root and cause from which arise all injuries to our neighbors... Above all, he wants the heart to be pure, even though, as long as we live here, we cannot accomplish that. So this commandment remains, like all the rest, one that constantly accuses us and shows just how upright we really are in God's sight.

BIBLICAL WISDOM

But if you have bitter envy and selfish ambition in your hearts, do not be boastful and false to the truth. Such wisdom does not come down from above, but is earthly, unspiritual, devilish. For where there is envy and selfish ambition, there will also be disorder and wickedness of every kind. But the wisdom from above is first pure, then peaceable, gentle, willing to yield, full of mercy and good fruits, without a trace of partiality or hypocrisy. James 3:14-17

SILENCE FOR MEDITATION

Questions to Ponder

- Why do you think Luther calls covetousness "miserable"?
- Greed, envy, and covetousness are all around. How can our faith help us to counteract this reality?
- Why does Luther see helping the neighbor as so important to the Ten Commandments?

Psalm Fragment

The righteous will see, and fear,
and will laugh at the evildoer, saying,
"See the one who would not take
refuge in God,
but trusted in abundant riches,
and sought refuge in wealth!" Psalm 52:6-7

Journal Reflections

- Envy is often pictured as a green-eyed monster. As you examine yourself, write about what if any role this green-eyed monster plays in your own life.
- Would you describe yourself as content or envious of others? Are you satisfied or covetous? Explain.
- Meditate on what it would mean to have a pure heart. Luther says we can't accomplish it on our own. Do you think that is true? How would one go about seeking a pure heart?

Prayers for the Life of Faith

Pray for those who may be consumed with envy so much that they cannot be freed from it. Ask that you would have the courage to speak to your relative or friend about the problem.

Prayer for Today

O Lord Jesus, come into my heart and purify it, cleanse it from envy and covetousness, and help me to live in gratitude for what I have.

Notes

NOW, AS WE SAID BEFORE, these words (the Ten Commandants) contain both a wrathful threat and a friendly promise, not only to terrify and warn us but also to attract and allure us, so that we will receive and regard God's Word as seriously as he does. For God declares how important the commandments are to him and how strictly he will watch over them, namely that he will fearfully and terribly punish all who despise and transgress his commandments; and again, how richly he will reward, bless, and bestow all good things on those who prize them and gladly act and live in accordance with them. Thus he demands that all our actions proceed from a heart that fears God, looks to him alone, and because of this fear avoids all that is contrary to his will, lest he be moved to wrath. Conversely, he demands that our actions proceed from a heart that trusts in him alone and for his sake does all that he asks of us, because he reveals himself as a kind father and offers us every grace and blessing.

BIBLICAL WISDOM

Do not think that I have come to abolish the law or the prophets; I have come not to abolish but to fulfill. For truly I tell you, until heaven and earth pass away, not one letter, not one stroke of a letter, will pass from the law until all is accomplished. Whoever then annuls one of the least of these commandments, and so teaches others, shall be called least in the kingdom of heaven; but whoever keeps and teaches them, he shall be called great in the kingdom of heaven. Matthew 5:17-19

SILENCE FOR MEDITATION

QUESTIONS TO PONDER

- Are the commandments a cause of terror, a means of grace, or both? Explain.

- Is it possible to have a heart that "trusts" in God alone? If so, how is such a heart developed and nurtured? If not, why not?
- How might a community of faith help us come to know that the law is kind and God is a kind father, as Luther says?

Psalm Fragment

O Lord, who may abide in your tent?
Who may dwell on your holy hill?
Those who walk blamelessly, and do what is right,
  and speak the truth from their heart;
  who do not slander with their tongue,
  and do no evil to their friends,
  nor take up a reproach against their neighbors. Psalm 15:1-3

Journal Reflections

- Do you experience God's law primarily as a "wrathful threat" or "a friendly promise"? Explain.
- Meditate in writing on how you imagine God to be. What are your primary images of God? How do these images shape your faith and your life in the world?
- Meditate on whether you "receive and regard God's word as seriously as he does." Does your meditation suggest any changes you might need to make?

Prayers for the Life of Faith

Pray that you and others in your community will try to live as God has commanded so that life will flourish and you may walk blamelessly in the grace of our Lord Jesus Christ.

Prayer for Today

Dear Lord Jesus, you came to be the fulfillment of the law and to give me life. Make my heart pure and obedient to you.

Notes

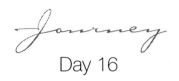

Day 16

WE ARE TO KEEP THEM [the Ten Commandments] incessantly before our eyes and constantly in our memory and to practice them in all our works and ways. Each of us is to make them a matter of daily practice in all circumstances, in all activities and dealings, as if they were written everywhere we look, even wherever we go or wherever we stand. Thus, both for ourselves at home and abroad among our neighbors, we will find occasion enough to practice the Ten Commandments, and no one need search far for them.

BIBLICAL WISDOM

Keep these words that I am commanding you today in your heart. Recite them to your children and talk about them when you are at home and when you are away, when you lie down and when you rise. Bind them as a sign on your hand, fix them as an emblem on your forehead, And you shall write them on the doorposts of your house and on your gates. Deuteronomy 6:6-9

SILENCE FOR MEDITATION

QUESTIONS TO PONDER

- There are many places in Scripture that tell us that the law is to be meditated on day and night, e.g., Psalm 1:1-2; Psalm 119:97; Joshua 1:8. What does that mean to you?
- What difference might it make to memorize the Ten Commandments and recite them daily? Why not do it?
- Read Romans 13:8-10 and Matthew 22:36-40. What is the relationship between the Ten Commandments and love?

Psalm Fragment

With my whole heart I cry;
  answer me, O Lord.
I will keep your statutes.
I cry to you; save me,
  that I may observe your decrees.
I rise before dawn and cry for help;
  I put my hope in your words. Psalm 119:145-47

Journal Reflections

- Meditate in writing on whether the commandments are true guides to your own life.
- Write about what you have learned so far about God from Luther's writings on the commandments and the biblical passages that have accompanied them.
- Make a list of any changes you want to make after having meditated on the commandments. How will you start to make these changes?

Prayers for the Life of Faith

Pray that you might always live by these words and that those around you may as well.

Prayer for Today

Dear Lord Jesus, teach me your way that I may not depart from it today and forever. Forgive me when I fail and restore me to your grace and love daily.

Notes

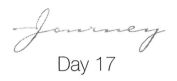

Day 17

THUS FAR WE HAVE HEARD the first part of Christian teaching, and in it we have seen all that God wishes us to do and not to do. The Creed properly follows, which sets forth all that we must expect and receive from God, in short, it teaches us to know him perfectly. It is given in order to help us do what the Ten Commandments require of us. For, as we said above, they are set so high that all human ability is far too puny and weak to keep them. Therefore it is just as necessary to learn this part as it is the other so that we may know where and how to obtain the power to do this. If we were able by our own strength to keep the Ten Commandments as they ought to be kept, we would need nothing else, neither the Creed nor the Lord's Prayer.

BIBLICAL WISDOM

And Jesus came and said to them, "All authority in heaven and on earth has been given to me. Go therefore and make disciples of all nations, baptizing them in the name of the Father and of the Son and of the Holy Spirit, and teaching them to obey everything that I have commanded you. And remember, I am with you always, to the end of the age." Matthew 28:18-20

SILENCE FOR MEDITATION

QUESTIONS TO PONDER

- How does the focus on the Apostles' Creed follow from the Ten Commandments?
- What is Luther's logic for putting the Creed after the Ten Commandments in the Catechism?
- Teaching what Jesus has commanded us is part of Jesus' Great Commission to his followers. What exactly is it that we are supposed to teach? (See Matthew 22:36-40 and John 13:24-35.) How is this teaching to be done?

PSALM FRAGMENT

My soul is satisfied as with a rich feast,
and my mouth praises you with joyful lips
when I think of you on my bed,
and meditate on you in the watches of the night;
for you have been my help,
and in the shadow of your wings I sing for joy. Psalm 63:5-7

JOURNAL REFLECTIONS

- Write about how it feels to change the focus of your meditations from what God would have you do to the nature of God.
- Say the Apostles' Creed aloud and reflect on what strikes you as you say it. Write about what in the Creed is easy for you to believe and what is difficult to believe. Explain.
- Read Psalm 63:1-3. Do you hunger as the Psalmist does to know God better? Meditate on this hunger. In what ways is this 40-day journey with Martin Luther helping to satisfy your longing?

PRAYERS FOR THE LIFE OF FAITH

Pray that you will come to understand better any difficulties you may have with the Creed during the next few days.

PRAYER FOR TODAY

Gracious God, open my mind and heart, my body and soul, to the knowledge of you and your great salvation so that I may live more fully and deeply in your love and grace.

NOTES

Journey

Day 18

I BELIEVE IN GOD, THE Father almighty, Creator of heaven and earth.

This is the shortest possible way of describing and illustrating the nature, will, acts, and work of God the Father. Because the Ten Commandments have explained that we are to have no more than one God, so it may now be asked, "What kind of person is God? What does he do? How can we praise or portray or describe him in such a way so we may know him?" This is taught here and in the following articles. Thus the Creed is nothing else than a response and confession of Christians based on the First Commandment. If you were to ask a young child, "My dear, what kind of God do you have? What do you know about him?" he or she could say: "First, my God is the Father, who made heaven and earth. Aside from this one alone I regard nothing as God, for there is no one else who could create heaven and earth."

BIBLICAL WISDOM

In the beginning when God created the heavens and the earth, the earth was a formless void and darkness covered the face of the deep, while a wind from God swept over the face of the waters. Genesis 1:1-2

SILENCE FOR MEDITATION

QUESTIONS TO PONDER

- What does it mean to "confess" one's faith? Is confession only a matter of words?
- In a world troubled by increasingly serious environmental and ecological questions, what does it mean to confess faith in a God who is the "Creator of heaven and earth"?
- Why is it important that children have a simple (and yet profound) way to answer the question "What kind of God do you have?"

Psalm Fragment

By the word of the Lord the heavens were made,
and all their host by the breath of his mouth...
Let all the earth fear the Lord;
let all the inhabitants of the world stand in awe of him.
For he spoke, and it came to be;
he commanded, and it stood firm. Psalm 33:6-9

Journal Reflections

- Meditate on Luther's questions: "What kind of God do you have? What do you know about him?" Answer the questions for yourself in your journal.
- Write about how your understanding of God shapes your daily life.
- Is your prayer life impacted by the wonder of God's creation which surrounds you on all sides? If yes, how? If not, meditate on creation and see where it takes you.

Prayers for the Life of Faith

Pray that you may come to know God better through this 40-day journey and that you will be able to share with someone your great wonder at the God who created all things.

Prayer for Today

Dear Heavenly Father, I thank you for all that you have done to create, sustain, and preserve all that is so that I might live a full life here on earth, serving you and your creation as obediently as I am able.

Notes

Day 19

I BELIEVE THAT GOD HAS created me together with all that exists. God has given me and still preserves my body and soul; eyes, ears, and all limbs and senses; reason and all mental faculties. In addition, God daily and abundantly provides shoes and clothing, food and drink, house and farm, spouse and children, fields, livestock, and all property—along with all the necessities and nourishment for this body and life. God protects me against all danger and shields and preserves me from all evil. And all this is done out of pure, fatherly, and divine goodness and mercy, without any merit or worthiness of mine at all! For all of this I owe it to God to thank and praise, serve and obey him. This is most certainly true.

If we believe it, this article should humble and terrify all of us. For we sin daily with eyes, ears, hands, body and soul, money and property, and with all that we have, especially those who even fight against the Word of God. Yet Christians have this advantage, that they acknowledge that they owe it to God to serve and obey him for all these things.

BIBLICAL WISDOM

Thus says God, the LORD, who created the heavens and stretched them out, who spread out the earth and what comes from it, who gives breath to the people upon it and spirit to those who walk in it: "I am the LORD, I have called you in righteousness, I have taken you by the hand and kept you; I have given you as a covenant to the people, a light to the nations, to open the eyes that are blind, to bring out the prisoners from the dungeon, from the prison those who sit in darkness." Isaiah 42:5-7

SILENCE FOR MEDITATION

QUESTIONS TO PONDER

- If "God daily and abundantly provides…all the necessities and nourishment for this body and life," why is it that so many are poor, hungry, and lacking the abundant life?

- In what way does confessing faith in the "creator of heaven and earth" make us a "light to the nations"?
- What kind of advantage do Christians have in knowing what they owe to God?

Psalm Fragment

When I look at your heavens, the work of your fingers,
the moon and the stars that you have established;
what are human beings that you are mindful of them,
mortals that you care for them? Psalm 8:3-4

Journal Reflections

- Make a list of what God has given you and for which you owe God praise, service, and obedience. In what ways are you giving to God what you owe God? What more might you (should you) be doing?
- Meditate on today's *Psalm Fragment*. Write about any feelings or thoughts the reading evokes in you.
- Reflect on times when you have seen some great evidence of God's creative power. Write a short poem to express your feelings.

Prayers for the Life of Faith

Pray that your eyes will be opened to see the greatness of God in the grandeur of creation and also in the little gifts you receive from family and friends.

Prayer for Today

Dear Creator, Redeemer, and Comforter, open my eyes to your grandeur in all the gifts you have given me abundantly. Help me to love, serve, and praise you forever.

Notes

Day 20

AND I BELIEVE IN JESUS Christ, his only Son, our Lord, who was conceived by the Holy Spirit, born of the Virgin Mary, suffered under Pontius Pilate, was crucified, died, and was buried; he descended into hell. On the third day he rose again; he ascended into heaven, seated at the right hand of God, the almighty Father, from where he will come to judge the living and the dead.

When we were created by God the Father and had received from him all kinds of good things, the devil came and led us into disobedience, sin, death, and all misfortune. As a result, we lay under God's wrath and displeasure, sentenced to eternal damnation, as we had merited it and deserved it. There was no counsel, no help, no comfort for us until this only and eternal Son of God, in his unfathomable goodness, had mercy on us because of our misery and distress and came from heaven to help us. Those tyrants and jailers have now been routed, and their place has been taken by Jesus Christ, the Lord of life, righteousness, and every good and blessing. He has snatched us, poor lost creatures, from the jaws of hell, won us, made us free, and restored us to the Father's favor and grace. As his own possession he has taken us under his protection and shelter, in order that he may rule us by his righteousness, wisdom, power, life, and blessedness.

BIBLICAL WISDOM

God proves his love for us in that while we still were sinners Christ died for us. Much more surely then, now that we have been justified by his blood, will we be saved through him from the wrath of God. For if while we were enemies, we were reconciled to God through the death of his Son, much more surely, having been reconciled, will we be saved by his life. Romans 5:8-10

SILENCE FOR MEDITATION

QUESTIONS TO PONDER

• Note the very strong sense of conflict between good and evil, Christ and the devil, in Luther. Where do you think the human being is in this battle?

If you have a hymnal with you, read and meditate on Luther's *A Mighty Fortress Is Our God.*

- What kind of freedom do we receive from Christ's victory? How is this worked out in our daily lives?
- What does it mean to say that Christ rules us by "righteousness, wisdom, power, life and blessedness"?

PSALM FRAGMENT

Bless the LORD, O my soul,
*   and do not forget all his benefits—*
who forgives all your iniquity,
who heals all your diseases,
who redeems your life from the Pit,
who crowns you with steadfast love and mercy... Psalm 103:2-4

JOURNAL REFLECTIONS

- Meditate on the struggle between good and evil, Christ and the devil, in your own life. Does it seem real to you? Do you sense it daily? How?
- Journal about the ways in which public worship and private devotion reassure you of Christ's victory and empower you to live in the freedom Christ gives.
- Write about the ways in which you experience Christ's power and presence in moments of weakness, failure, fear, or doubt. Is there anything you might do to better avail yourself of Christ's power and presence at all times?

PRAYERS FOR THE LIFE OF FAITH

Pray that you may claim daily the victory of Jesus over "sin, death, and the devil," and that you may help those around you to hear the good news that in Christ there is hope and victory.

PRAYER FOR TODAY

Lord Jesus, I thank you for all your many blessings to me. Help me to claim your promises all through the day today no matter the difficulties I may face.

NOTES

I BELIEVE THAT JESUS CHRIST, true God, begotten of the Father in eternity, and also a true human being, born of the Virgin Mary, is my LORD. He has redeemed me, a lost and condemned human being. He has purchased and freed me from all sins, from death, and from the power of the devil, not with gold or silver but with his holy, precious blood and with his innocent suffering and death. He has done all this in order that I may belong to him, live under him in his kingdom, and serve him in eternal righteousness, innocence, and blessedness, just as he is risen from the dead and lives and rules eternally. This is most certainly true.

Let this be the summary of this article, that the little word "LORD" simply means the same as Redeemer, that is, he who has brought us back from the devil to God, from death to life, from sin to righteousness, and keeps us there… Indeed, the entire gospel that we preach depends on the proper understanding of this article. Upon it all our salvation and blessedness are based, and it is so rich and broad that we can never learn it fully.

BIBLICAL WISDOM

What then are we to say about these things? If God is for us, who is against us? He who did not withhold his own Son, but gave him up for all of us, will he not with him also give us everything else? Who will bring any charge against God's elect? It is God who justifies. Who is to condemn? It is Christ Jesus, who died, yes, who was raised, who is at the right hand of God, who indeed intercedes for us. Romans 8:31-33

SILENCE FOR MEDITATION

QUESTIONS TO PONDER

- Why did God have to go to such lengths to save us? Was the death of Christ necessary? If yes, why? If no, why not?

- People prize their independence. Does that make it difficult to say "I belong to Christ?"
- When do we start to "live under him in his kingdom, and serve him in eternal righteousness, innocence, and blessedness"? Now, in this life? In the next life? Both now and then? Explain.

Psalm Fragment

Blessed be the LORD,
who daily bears us up;
God is our salvation.
Our God is a God of salvation,
and to GOD, the LORD, belongs escape from death. Psalm 68:19-20

Journal Reflections

- Write on what it means for you to have a Lord, or Redeemer, in your own life.
- Do you remember a time when you felt as though Christ had snatched you from death and brought you back to God, or from sin to righteousness? If so, write about the experience. If not, can you imagine such an experience?
- If someone asked you what is "the entire gospel," how would you answer?

Prayers for the Life of Faith

Thank God for the great gift of Jesus for you and pray that you and others you know will come to understand more deeply and fully the depths of this gift.

Prayer for Today

Lord Jesus, I thank you that you have, through great suffering and sacrifice, redeemed me from death, sin, and the power of the devil. Keep your grace ever before me today as I live and work in your world.

Notes

Journey

Day 22

I BELIEVE IN THE HOLY Spirit, one holy Christian church, the community of saints, forgiveness of sins, resurrection of the flesh, and eternal life. Amen.

To this article, as I have said, I cannot give a better title than "Being Made Holy." In it are expressed and portrayed the Holy Spirit and his office, which is that he makes us holy. Therefore, we must concentrate on the term "HOLY SPIRIT," because it is so precise we can find no substitute for it… God's Spirit alone is called a Holy Spirit, that is, the one who has made us holy and still makes us holy. As the Father is called a Creator and the Son is called a Redeemer, so on account of his work the Holy Spirit must be called a Sanctifier, or one who makes us holy. How does such sanctifying take place? Answer:… the Holy Spirit effects our being made holy through the following: the community of saints or Christian Church, the forgiveness of sins, the resurrection of the body, and the life everlasting. That is, he first leads us into his holy community, placing us in the church's lap, where he preaches to us and brings us to Christ.

ے

BIBLICAL WISDOM

When the Spirit of truth comes, he will guide you into all the truth; for he will not speak on his own, but will speak whatever he hears, and he will declare to you the things that are to come. He will glorify me, because he will take what is mine and declare it to you. All that the Father has is mine. For this reason I said that he will take what is mine and declare it to you. John 16:13-15

SILENCE FOR MEDITATION

QUESTIONS TO PONDER

- What do you think Luther means when he says the Holy Spirit is the "one who makes us holy"? What does it mean to be made holy?

- Luther says the Spirit "effects our being made holy" through "the community of saints or Christian Church, the forgiveness of sins, the resurrection of the body, and the life everlasting." Reflect on these four; how do they make us holy?
- According to today's reading from Luther, what is the church's primary task? Why?

PSALM FRAGMENT

These all look to you
to give them their food in due season;
when you give to them, they gather it up;
when you open your hand, they are filled with good things.
When you hide your face, they are dismayed;
when you take away their breath, they die
and return to their dust.
When you send forth your spirit, they are created;
and you renew the face of the ground. Psalm 104:27-30

JOURNAL REFLECTIONS

- Meditate in writing on your understanding and experience of the Holy Spirit.
- Have you ever felt as if the Holy Spirit was bringing Christ to you as you studied his word or heard it preached, or participated in the activities of his church? If so, write about the experience and its impact on you.
- Have you experienced yourself "being made holy"? If so, has it changed how you make decisions? How you live in relationships? If not, can you imagine "being made holy" and its consequences?

PRAYERS FOR THE LIFE OF FAITH

Pray that your relationship with God through Christ and the Holy Spirit will become more dear to you and that the gift of faith you have received will flow from you into good deeds for your family, friends, and neighbors.

PRAYER FOR TODAY

Come, Holy Spirit, teach me more about God, and quicken my love for you and my neighbors so that I may serve you as I should by serving them.

NOTES

I BELIEVE THAT BY MY own understanding or strength I cannot believe in Jesus Christ my Lord or come to him, but instead the Holy Spirit has called me through the gospel, enlightened me with his gifts, made me holy and kept me in the true faith, just as he calls, gathers, enlightens and makes holy the whole Christian church on earth and keeps it with Jesus Christ in the one common, true faith.

Because holiness has begun and is growing daily, we await the time when our flesh will be put to death, will be buried with all its uncleanness, and will come forth gloriously and arise to complete and perfect holiness in a new, eternal life. Now, however, we remain only halfway pure and holy. The Holy Spirit must always work in us through the Word, granting us daily forgiveness until we attain to that life where there will be no more forgiveness. In that life there will be only perfectly pure and holy people, full of integrity and righteousness, completely freed from sin, death, and all misfortune, living in new, immortal, and glorified bodies.

BIBLICAL WISDOM

I consider that the sufferings of this present time are not worth comparing with the glory about to be revealed to us. Romans 8:18

SILENCE FOR MEDITATION

QUESTIONS TO PONDER

- If, as Luther suggests, both the capacity to believe and the content of our faith are pure gifts of grace given by the Holy Spirit, what—if any—is the role of human effort in our relationship with God?
- Why is the *daily* forgiveness of sins so central to the work of the Holy Spirit?

- What does it mean to say that "the Holy Spirit must always work in us through the Word?"

PSALM FRAGMENT

Create in me a clean heart, O God,
  and put a new and right spirit within me.
Do not cast me away from your presence,
  and do not take your holy spirit from me.
Restore to me the joy of your salvation,
  and sustain in me a willing spirit. Psalm 51:10-12

JOURNAL REFLECTIONS

- Have you experienced a longing to be "perfectly pure and holy"? If so, describe the longing in your journal. How has this longing impacted your life? If not, can you imagine what it might be like to have such a longing?
- How often do your read the Bible and spend time in prayer? Does it feel like enough time?
- Do your devotional practices sharpen both your sense of sin and your joy in God's forgiveness?

PRAYERS FOR THE LIFE OF FAITH

Pray that your congregation will faithfully preach Christ in the power of the Holy Spirit so that more will be called, gathered, enlightened, and sanctified in the one true faith.

PRAYER FOR TODAY

Come, O Holy Spirit, enliven my faith today, show me the depth of my sins and the glory I receive in the forgiveness of my sins.

NOTES

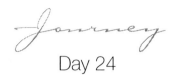

BEFORE WE EXPLAIN THE LORD'S Prayer part by part, the most necessary thing is to exhort and encourage people to pray, as Christ and the apostles also did. The first thing to know is this: It is our duty to pray because of God's command. For we heard in the Second Commandment, "You are not to take God's name in vain." Thereby we are required to praise the holy name and to pray or call upon it in every need. For calling upon it is nothing else than praying. Prayer, therefore, is as strictly and solemnly commanded as all the other commandments...lest anyone thinks it makes no difference whether I pray or not...

BIBLICAL WISDOM

Ask, and it shall be given to you; seek, and you shall find; knock, and it shall be opened to you. For everyone who asks receives, and everyone who searches finds, and for everyone who knocks, the door will be opened Is there anyone among you who, if your child asks for bread, will give a stone? Or if the child asks for a fish, will give a snake? If you then, who are evil, know how to give good gifts to your children, how much more will your Father in heaven give good things to those who ask him! Matthew 7:7-11

SILENCE FOR MEDITATION

QUESTIONS TO PONDER

- Why is our prayer so important to God? What is the good news in the duty or command to pray?
- Read these places in Scripture that exhort and encourage people to pray: Matthew 7:7, Luke 18:1, 21:36, Romans 12:12, Philippians 4:4-7, Colossians 4:2, 1 Thessalonians 5:16-19. What do they all have in common? What are the implications for an individual's life of faith and for life together in the community of faith?

- What picture does Jesus give us of prayer in the Matthew passage above? Does it fit with the Luther reading? How or how not?

PSALM FRAGMENT

Hear my cry, O God;
*   listen to my prayer.*
From the end of the earth I call to you,
*   when my heart is faint.*
Lead me to the rock
*   that is higher than I;*
for you are my refuge,
*   a strong tower against the enemy.* Psalm 61:1-3

JOURNAL REFLECTIONS

- Journal about your understanding of prayer and its place in your life.
- What do you pray about? Have you ever kept a prayer list to remind you of who and what to pray for? If yes, how has it worked for you? If not, why not start one now?
- Reflect on when and how you pray. Are you happy with the way you pray? If yes, why? If not, why not?

PRAYERS FOR THE LIFE OF FAITH

Pray that you can come to relish your time of prayer and learn to approach God with everything, as Christ instructs us to do.

PRAYER FOR TODAY

Gracious God, come now to me as I cry out to you and seek your presence. Fill me with your Holy Spirit and give me life and salvation.

NOTES

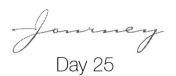

Day 25

WE SHOULD BE ENCOURAGED AND drawn to pray [the Lord's Prayer] because…God takes the initiative and puts into our mouths the very words and approach we are to use. In this way we see how deeply concerned he is about our needs, and we should never doubt that such prayer pleases him and will assuredly be heard. So this prayer is far superior to all others that we might devise ourselves. For in that case our conscience would always be in doubt, saying, "I have prayed, but who knows whether it pleases him or whether I have hit upon the right form and mode?" Thus there is no nobler prayer to be found on earth, for it has the powerful testimony that God loves to hear it.

BIBLICAL WISDOM

And will not God grant justice to his chosen ones who cry to him day and night? Will he delay long in helping them? I tell you, he will quickly grant justice to them. Luke 18:7-8

SILENCE FOR MEDITATION

QUESTIONS TO PONDER

- According to Luther, why is the Lord's Prayer superior to all others? Do you agree with him? Why or why not?
- The Lord's Prayer is very familiar to all Christians. It is said that "familiarity breeds contempt." What can individuals (and churches) do to keep the Prayer alive and fresh with meaning?
- How seriously is prayer taken in your community of faith? Are there other ways prayer might be emphasized and practiced by your faith community? Who should you talk to about it?

Psalm Fragment

I cry aloud to God,
aloud to God, that he may hear me.
In the day of my trouble I seek the Lord;
in the night my hand is stretched out without wearying;
my soul refuses to be comforted. Psalm 77:1-2

Journal Reflections

- Meditate on the Lord's Prayer, then write a few lines for each petition explaining what it means to you right now.
- Read the Luther passage for Journey Day 5 again. Luther advises that in prayer you should "open and spread your apron wide to receive many things." What do you think that means? Have you ever done that? If so, what was your experience like? If not, why not try it?
- Write about your experience with answers to prayer.

Prayers for the Life of Faith

Pray that you will be given the freedom to lament, praise, ask, importune God in your prayers, bringing everything in your life before him.

Prayer for Today

Holy and Righteous God, I come to you today because you have commanded me to. Give me the grace and courage to bring everything before you so I can open myself to receiving all that you have to give.

Notes

Journey

Day 26

MAY YOUR NAME BE HALLOWED.

What is this?

Answer: It is true that God's name is holy in itself, but we ask in this prayer that it may also become holy in and among us.

But what is it to pray that his name may become holy? Is it not already holy? Answer: Yes, in its essence it is always holy, but our use of it is not holy. God's name was given to us when we became Christians and were baptized, and so we are called children of God and have the sacrament, through which he incorporates us into himself with the result that everything that is God's must serve for our use. Thus it is a matter of grave necessity, about which we should be most concerned that God's name receive due honor and be kept holy and sacred as the greatest treasure and most sacred thing that we have, and that, as good children, we pray that his name, which is in any case holy in heaven, may also be holy and be kept holy on earth in our midst and in all the world.

BIBLICAL WISDOM

Like obedient children, do not be conformed to the desires that you formerly had in ignorance. Instead, as he who called you is holy, be holy yourselves in all your conduct; for it is written, "You shall be holy, for I am holy." 1 Peter 1:14-16

SILENCE FOR MEDITATION

QUESTIONS TO PONDER

- What does it mean for God's name to be "holy in and among us"?
- In what ways might our lives and communities change if God's name was truly holy "in our midst and in all the world"?
- What does it mean to say that "everything that is God's must serve for our use"? If this is true, what does it have to say about how we should be in the world?

PSALM FRAGMENT

Blessed be the LORD, the God of Israel,
who alone does wondrous things.
Blessed be his glorious name forever;
may his glory fill the whole earth.
Amen and Amen. Psalm 72:18-19

JOURNAL REFLECTIONS

- Today's *Biblical Wisdom* tells us "*as he who called you is holy, be holy your-selves in all your conduct.*" Write about what you think God's holiness is. Write about the implications of God's holiness for the way you try to live.
- Reflect in writing on what you do in your day to day living that "hallows' God's name. Any behaviors that need to stop, change, or be added?
- In a list of all the "treasures" you have, where would you rank "God's name"? Why?

PRAYERS FOR THE LIFE OF FAITH

Pray that you may be given help to hallow God's name in your speech and actions, and give thanks that because of your relationship with Christ, you have been made holy.

PRAYER FOR TODAY

Our Father in heaven, hallowed be your name! Thank you that your holiness also has made me holy. Although I do not understand, nor do I feel holy, keep me Lord always near to your holiness and love.

NOTES

Journey

Day 27

MAY YOUR NAME BE HALLOWED.

How does this come about?

Whenever the Word of God is taught clearly and purely and we, as God's children, also live holy lives according to it.

So you see that in this petition we pray for exactly the same thing that God demands in the Second Commandment: that his name should not be taken in vain by swearing, cursing, deceiving, etc., but used rightly to the praise and glory of God. Whoever uses God's name for any sort of wrong profanes and desecrates this holy name…thus rendering unholy by misuse that which is holy in itself. This petition, then, is simple and clear if we only understand the language, namely, that to "hallow" means the same as in our idiom "to praise, extol, and honor" both in word and deed.

BIBLICAL WISDOM

When you are praying, do not heap up empty phrases as the Gentiles do; for they think that they will be heard because of their many words. Do not be like them, for your Father knows what you need before you ask him. Matthew 6:7-8

SILENCE FOR MEDITATION

QUESTIONS TO PONDER

- Luther insists that God's name is "hallowed" when "we, as God's children,… live holy lives according to it (God's word)." What would such a life look like?
- In what ways does teaching and living contrary to the word of God profane the name of God?
- In what ways might a church which "hallows" God's name, that is, which seeks "to praise, extol, and honor" God "both in word and deed," be countercultural?

Journal Reflections

- Think back to times when you experienced someone misusing the name of God carelessly or for false or malicious purposes. How did you feel and how did you respond?
- Think back. Have you ever been indifferent to God's holiness? If so, describe the feeling. If not, what helps to keep you focused?
- Write down ways in which you will try "to praise, extol, and honor" God "both in word and deed," today. How can you encourage others to do the same?

Prayers for the Life of Faith

Pray that the word of God will be preached and kept purely in your own congregation, and pray that you can find ways to share the word with one person you know who is longing to hear the Gospel.

Prayer for Today

Holy Lord, I bow before you with awe and wonder that you have gone to such great lengths for me, a poor sinner, and given your own Son to make me yours.

Notes

MAY YOUR KINGDOM COME.

What does this mean?

In fact, God's kingdom comes on its own without our prayer, but we ask in this prayer that it may also come to us.

What is the kingdom of God? Answer: Simply what we heard above in the Creed, namely, that God sent his Son, Christ our Lord, into the world to redeem and deliver us from the power of the devil, to bring us to himself, and to rule us as a king of righteousness, life, and salvation against sin, death, and an evil conscience. To this end, he also gave his Holy Spirit to deliver this to us through his holy Word and to enlighten and strengthen us in faith by his power. We ask here at the outset, that all this may be realized in us and that his name may be praised through God's holy Word and Christian living. This we ask, both in order that we who have accepted it may remain faithful and grow daily in it and also in order that it may find approval and gain followers among other people and advance with power through the world.

BIBLICAL WISDOM

He put before them another parable: "The kingdom of heaven is like a mustard seed that someone took and sowed in his field; it is the smallest of all the seeds, but when it has grown it is the greatest of shrubs and becomes a tree, so that the birds of the air come and make nests in its branches." Matthew 13:31-32

SILENCE FOR MEDITATION

QUESTIONS TO PONDER

- What does it mean to say that God's kingdom is invisible, or at least difficult to see, like the tiny mustard seed in Jesus' parables?
- How do we "remain faithful and grow daily" in God's kingdom?

- If God's kingdom is the redemptive work of Christ culminating in his "rule [over] us as a king of righteousness, life, and salvation against sin, death, and evil," what does this mean for the mission of the church in the world?

PSALM FRAGMENT

They shall speak of the glory of your kingdom,
and tell of your power,
to make known to all people your mighty deeds,
and the glorious splendor of your kingdom. Psalm 145:11-12

JOURNAL REFLECTIONS

- Journal on what it means to you to live under the rule (or in the kingdom) of God?
- Write about the ways in which you sense the Holy Spirit advancing the reign and rule of God in your life and in the world?
- Make a list of the ways in which you might be a part of the Spirit's work in advancing God's rule in the world.

PRAYERS FOR THE LIFE OF FAITH

Pray for someone you know who seems not to be among those who believe. Pray that you can speak the right word, and sow the seed in them.

PRAYER FOR TODAY

Gracious God, I pray that you will give me the courage to speak your word and live according to your word where it is needed, and the patience to wait for your harvest.

NOTES

MAY YOUR KINGDOM COME.

How does this come about?

Whenever our heavenly Father gives us his Holy Spirit, so that through his grace we believe his Holy Word and live godly lives here in time and hereafter in eternity.

[God] desires nothing more from us than that we ask many and great things of him. And, on the contrary, he is angered if we do not ask and demand with confidence. Imagine if the richest and most powerful emperor commanded a poor beggar to ask for whatever he might desire and was prepared to give lavish, royal gifts, and the fool asked only for a dish of beggar's broth. He would rightly be considered a rogue and a scoundrel, who had made a mockery of the imperial majesty's command and was unworthy to come into his presence. Just so, it is a great reproach and dishonor to God if we, to whom he offers and pledges so many inexpressible blessings, despise them or lack confidence that we shall receive them and scarcely venture to ask for a morsel of bread.

BIBLICAL WISDOM

Do not be afraid, little flock, for it is your Father's good pleasure to give you the kingdom. Sell your possessions, and give alms. Make purses for yourselves that do not wear out, an unfailing treasure in heaven, where no thief comes near and no moth destroys. Luke 12:32-33

SILENCE FOR MEDITATION

QUESTIONS TO PONDER

• Why is it "a great reproach and dishonor to God" when we "lack confidence" that God will provide for us and fail to ask for all that we are commanded to ask for?

- Jesus speaks of the Father's "good pleasure." Luther talks about God's anger. How would you put these two emotions together in your picture of God?
- Why is the beggar who demurs from asking God for anything not living a "godly life"?

Psalm Fragment

O taste and see that the LORD is good;
  happy are those who take refuge in him.
O fear the LORD, you his holy ones,
  for those who fear him have no want.
The young lions suffer want and hunger,
  but those who seek the LORD lack no good thing. Psalm 34:8-10

Journal Reflections

- Reflect on a time when you acted more like the poor beggar in your relationship with God, asking only for a little when you really wanted much more. Why did you refrain from asking more?
- Meditate on your image of God and how that affects your prayer life.
- Does it surprise you that your failure to ask for everything from God is a reproach or dishonoring of God? If so, reflect on how you might learn to honor God by presuming more from God.

Prayers for the Life of Faith

Think of some things you have wanted from God but did not dare ask for. Think of another who might also have the same timidity. Pray that you both will be given the grace to overcome your fear.

Prayer for Today

Good and gracious Lord, you are rich and I am poor. Send your Holy Spirit to befriend me so that I dare to come to you and ask for all things.

Notes

Journey

Day 30

MAY YOUR WILL COME ABOUT on earth as in heaven.

What is this? Answer:

In fact, God's good and gracious will comes about without our prayer, but we ask in this prayer that it may also come about in and among us.

So here also; although we have prayed for what is most necessary—for the gospel, for faith, and for the Holy Spirit, that he may govern us who have been redeemed from the power of the devil—we must also pray that God will cause his will to be done. If we try to hold these treasures fast, we will have to suffer an astonishing number of attacks and assaults from all who venture to hinder and thwart the fulfillment of the first two petitions.

BIBLICAL WISDOM

He came out and went, as was his custom, to the Mount of Olives; and the disciples followed him. When he reached the place, he said to them, "Pray that you may not come into the time of trial." Then he withdrew from them about a stone's throw, knelt down, and prayed, "Father, if you are willing, remove this cup from me; yet, not my will but yours be done." Luke 22:39-42

SILENCE FOR MEDITATION

QUESTIONS TO PONDER

- Why does holding fast to the treasures of the faith cause suffering and assaults?
- Jesus prays to be spared drinking the cup of suffering, but prays also that God's will be done. Why does the doing of God's will often involve so much suffering?
- Luther states that "God's good and gracious will comes about without our prayer." Why pray, then, that it be done "in and among us"?

PSALM FRAGMENT

The LORD has established his throne in the heavens,
*   and his kingdom rules over all.*
Bless the LORD, O you his angels,
*   you mighty ones who do his bidding,*
*   obedient to his spoken word.*
Bless the LORD, all his hosts,
*   his ministers that do his will.*
Bless the LORD, all his works,
*   in all places of his dominion.*
Bless the LORD, O my soul. Psalm 103:19-22

JOURNAL REFLECTIONS

- Have you ever felt you were suffering attacks from those powers or people that were trying to thwart the will of God? If so, write about what spiritual resources you were able to bring to the struggle. If not, what spiritual resources will you have if such an experience comes your way?
- Have you ever, like Jesus, prayed to have the cup of suffering pass from you? If so, write about the experience. If not, imagine what such an experience would be like.
- There are both joy and suffering for those who seek to follow God's will. Journal about the joy and suffering you have experienced in your faith life.

PRAYERS FOR THE LIFE OF FAITH

Pray that you can be obedient to God's will despite suffering. Remember a friend or member of your family who has suffered for the good, pray that they will be encouraged in their Christian journey.

PRAYER FOR TODAY

Dear Heavenly Father, I pray that your will be done in me and in my life. Show me how to follow your way to the end.

NOTES

Journey

Day 31

MAY YOUR WILL COME ABOUT on earth as in heaven.

How does this come about? Answer:

Whenever God breaks and hinders every evil scheme and will—as are present in the will of the devil, the world, and our flesh—that would not allow us to hallow God's name and would prevent the coming of his kingdom, and instead whenever God strengthens us and keeps us steadfast in his Word, and in faith until the end of our lives. This is his gracious and great will.

What we pray for concerns only ourselves in that…we ask that what otherwise must be done without us may also be done in us. Just as God's name must be hallowed and his kingdom must come even without our prayer, so must his will be done and prevail even though the devil and all his host bluster, storm, and rage furiously against it in their attempt to exterminate the gospel utterly. But we must pray for our own sake so that his will may be done also among us without hindrance, in spite of their fury, so that they may accomplish nothing and we may remain steadfast against all violence and persecution and submit to the will of God.

⁓

BIBLICAL WISDOM

But he knew what they were thinking and said to them, "Every kingdom divided against itself becomes a desert, and house falls on house. If Satan also is divided against himself, how will his kingdom stand?—for you say that I cast out the demons by Beelzebul. Now if I cast out the demons by Beelzebul, by whom do your exorcists cast them out? Therefore they will be your judges. But if it is by the finger of God that I cast out the demons, then the kingdom of God has come to you. Luke 11:17-20

SILENCE FOR MEDITATION

Questions to Ponder

- Luther understood that a Christian or church that seeks to be faithful to God's will can expect to experience "violence and persecution." Why is this so? What evidence of this do you see in the world?
- In what ways might a community of faith work together to discern the will of God for them?
- Can God's will ever be thwarted?

Psalm Fragment

Your way, O God, is holy.
What god is so great as our God?
You are the God who works wonders;
you have displayed your might among the peoples.
With your strong arm you redeemed your people,
the descendants of Jacob and Joseph. Psalm 77:13-15

Journal Reflections

- Write about how, in your own life, you try to discern the will of God.
- Have you ever prayed "Your will be done on earth as it is in heaven" as a source of courage and strength in resisting the "enemy" and following God's will? If so, write about the experience and if it was helpful. If not, write about whether it seems a useful spiritual practice. Why not try it?
- Have you ever found yourself working against God's will? If so, how did you come to realize it? If not, can you imagine yourself working against God's will?

Prayers for the Life of Faith

Pray that the will of God may also be done in you and ask forgiveness for times in which you may have, as a sinful creature, opposed God's will.

Prayer for Today

Almighty God, may your will be done on earth as in heaven, and may it also be done in me.

Notes

Journey

Day 32

GIVE US TODAY OUR DAILY bread.

What is this?

Answer: In fact, God gives daily bread without our prayer, even to all evil people, but we ask in this prayer that God cause us to recognize what our daily bread is and to receive it with thanksgiving.

Here we consider the poor breadbasket—the needs of our body and our life on earth. It is a brief and simple word, but very comprehensive. When you say and ask for "daily bread," you ask for everything that is necessary in order to have and enjoy daily bread and, on the contrary, against everything that interferes with enjoying it. You must therefore expand and extend your thoughts to include not just the oven or the flour bin, but also the broad fields and the whole land that produce and provide our daily bread and all kinds of sustenance for us. For if God did not cause grain to grow and did not bless it and preserve it in the field, we could never have a loaf of bread to take from the oven or to set upon the table.

BIBLICAL WISDOM

Of course, there is great gain in godliness combined with contentment; for we brought nothing into the world, so that we can take nothing out of it; but if we have food and clothing, we will be content with these. 1 Timothy 6:6-8

SILENCE FOR MEDITATION

QUESTIONS TO PONDER

- For Luther, daily bread stands for everything that is necessary for life. How would you define the word "necessary?"
- Luther says that when we pray for daily bread we also pray "against everything that interferes with enjoying it." What does he mean?

- Luther says that, "God gives daily bread without our prayer, even to all evil people…" What does that tell us about God? (Compare Matthew 5:43-48)

PSALM FRAGMENT

You visit the earth and water it,
*   you greatly enrich it;*
*   the river of God is full of water;*
*   you provide the people with grain,*
*   for so you have prepared it.* Psalm 65:9

JOURNAL REFLECTIONS

- Make a list of all the good gifts you receive daily that make life both possible and good.
- Write down what you think is really "necessary" to life. Be sure to distinguish between "needs" and "wants."
- Read today's *Biblical Wisdom* again. With respect to material goods, are you usually contented or discontented? Explain.

PRAYERS FOR THE LIFE OF FAITH

Pray that God will continue to send good weather for the crops and animals you depend on for life and that you will remember to give thanks for the smallest gifts.

PRAYER FOR THE DAY

Good and gracious Lord, I thank you for your constant goodness to me, in providing me food, clothing, and shelter, all out of the things of the earth.

NOTES

Journey

Day 33

WHAT THEN DOES "DAILY BREAD" mean? Answer:

Everything included in the necessities and nourishment for our bodies, such as food, drink, clothing, shoes, house, farm, fields, livestock, money, property, an upright spouse, upright children, upright members of the household, upright and faithful rules, good government, good weather, peace, health, decency, honor, good friends, faithful neighbors, and the like.

But especially is this petition directed against our chief enemy, the devil, whose whole purpose and desire it is to take away or interfere with all we have received from God. He is not satisfied to obstruct and overthrow the spiritual order…but he also prevents and impedes the establishment of any kind of government or honorable and peaceful relations on earth… In short, it pains him that anyone should receive even a mouthful of bread from God and eat it in peace. If it were in his power and our prayer to God did not restrain him, surely we would not have a straw in the field, a penny in the house, or even an hour more of life—especially those of us who have the Word of God and would like to be Christians.

BIBLICAL WISDOM

Cast all your anxiety on him, because he cares for you. Discipline yourselves, keep alert. Like a roaring lion your adversary the devil prowls around, looking for someone to devour. 1 Peter 5:7-8

SILENCE FOR MEDITATION

QUESTIONS TO PONDER

- How do you think our prayer to God restrains the devil? Explain.
- Luther sees all of life on this earth as a battle between God and Satan concerning every single part of our lives, from spirit to flesh. What do you understand Luther to mean by this?

- Read again Luther's list of what constitutes "daily bread." What do you think is the responsibility of individual Christians and the church to see that all people enjoy this daily bread? How might this responsibility be worked out?

PSALM FRAGMENT

You cause the grass to grow for the cattle,
and plants for people to use,
to bring forth food from the earth,
and wine to gladden the human heart,
oil to make the face shine,
and bread to strengthen the human heart. Psalm 104:14-15

JOURNAL REFLECTIONS

- The Lord's Prayer directs us to ask: "Give us today our daily bread." Meditate on this petition and then write about what each of these words means to you.
- Make a list of all the things that might prevent you or anyone else from receiving and enjoying your "daily bread." Can you think of this petition as a way of saying "no" to these things? Why or why not?
- The concept of the "devil" was a common way to talk about evil and its consequences in Luther's time. Is Satan—or the devil—a reality for you? Explain. If not, how do you think about evil?

PRAYERS FOR THE LIFE OF FAITH

Pray that God will protect you and will triumph over the evil one, and give thanks for the good that God has done to give you a good life.

PRAYER FOR TODAY

Dear God, thank you for continuing to give us each day our daily bread; continue to give us the strength to stand against evil and teach us to be thankful.

NOTES

Journey

Day 34

AND REMIT OUR DEBTS, AS we remit what our debtors owe.

What is this?

Answer: We ask in this prayer that our heavenly Father would not regard our sins nor deny this petition on their account, for we are worthy of nothing for which we ask, nor have we earned it. Instead we ask that God would give us all things by grace, for we daily sin much and indeed deserve only punishment. So on the other hand, we, too, truly want to forgive heartily and to do good gladly to those who sin against us.

This sign ("as we forgive our debtors") is attached to the petition so that when we pray we may recall the promise and think, "Dear Father, I come to you and pray that you will forgive me for this reason: not because I can make satisfaction or deserve anything by my works, but because you have promised and have set this seal on it, making it as certain as if I had received an absolution pronounced by you yourself." For whatever baptism and the Lord's Supper, which are appointed to us as outward signs, can effect, this sign can as well, in order to strengthen and gladden our conscience. Moreover, above and beyond the other signs, it has been instituted precisely so that we can use and practice it every hour, keeping it with us at all times.

BIBLICAL WISDOM

We love because he first loved us. Those who say, "I love God," and hate their brothers or sisters, are liars; for those who do not love a brother or sister whom they have seen, cannot love God whom they have not seen. The commandment we have from him is this: those who love God must love their brothers and sisters also.
1 John 4:19-21

SILENCE FOR MEDITATION

Questions to Ponder

- Different versions of the Lord's Prayer use different words in this petition—sins, debts, trespasses. Which do you prefer? Why?
- What does the word "as" in this petition mean? Is our forgiveness conditional on our forgiving those who have sinned against us?
- How is our forgiving those who have sinned against us a "sign" like baptism or the Lord's Supper?

Psalm Fragment

If you, O LORD, should mark iniquities,
* Lord, who could stand?*
But there is forgiveness with you,
* so that you may be revered.* Psalm 130:3-4

Journal Reflections

- Meditate on whether forgiving others who have hurt or wronged you is easy or difficult for you.
- When you find it difficult or impossible to forgive another, what is the impact on your relationship with God?
- When Luther says that forgiving others is a "sign" he means that it is a sign of God's forgiveness of us. Luther tells us to "use and practice [this sign] every hour, keeping it with us at all times." Meditate on what it would be like to adopt forgiveness as a daily spiritual practice.

Prayers for the Life of Faith

Pray that you will be able to ask God for forgiveness and be able to forgive someone who has wounded you, and that they will also be willing to forgive you.

Prayer for Today

Dear Lord Jesus, you teach me to ask our Father for the forgiveness of my sins and to forgive those who have sinned against me. Give me the grace to do so.

Notes

Journey

Day 35

AND LEAD US NOT INTO temptation.

What is this?

Answer: It is true that God tempts no one, but we ask in this prayer that God would preserve and keep us, so that the devil, the world, and our flesh may not deceive us or mislead us into false belief, despair, and other great shame and vice, and that, although we may be attacked by them, we may finally prevail and gain the victory.

This, then, is what 'leading us not into temptation' means: when God gives us power and strength to resist, even though the attack is not removed or ended. For no one can escape temptations and allurements as long as we live in the flesh and have the devil prowling around us. We cannot help but suffer attacks, and even be mired in them, but we pray here that we may not fall into them and be drowned by them.

BIBLICAL WISDOM

He came out and went, as was his custom, to the Mount of Olives; and the disciples followed him. When he reached the place, he said to them, "Pray that you may not come into the time of trial." Luke 22:39-40

SILENCE FOR MEDITATION

QUESTIONS TO PONDER

- If "no one can escape temptations and allurements," how can a community of faith encourage and support people who are facing temptations and allurements?
- Is God ever the one who causes us to suffer? Explain.
- How can trials or temptations "prove" us? (See James 1:12-16.)

Psalm Fragment

Save me, O LORD, from my enemies;
I have fled to you for refuge.
Teach me to do your will,
for you are my God.
Let your good spirit lead me
on a level path. Psalm 143:9-10

Journal Reflections

- Have you ever felt God was against you, or at least absent? Write about the experience. How did you feel? How did you respond? What spiritual resources (or practices) did you have to help you through the experience?
- Describe a time when you fell into temptation. Reflect briefly on why you think that happened. Do you pray this petition each time you face "temptations and allurements"? If so, how does it work? If not, why not try it?
- Have you ever, by prayer and supplication, been able to defeat temptation? If so, write about the experience and what you learned from it. If not, how do you imagine prayer and supplication might be helpful in resisting temptation?

Prayers for the Life of Faith

Pray that you will continue to be kept from falling into sin and that you will be able to prevail against such temptations.

Prayer for Today

Dear heavenly Father, do not lead me into temptation. Save me in the time of trial and *"let your good spirit lead me on a level path."*

Notes

Journey

Day 36

BUT DELIVER US FROM EVIL.

What is this?

Answer: We ask in this prayer, as in a summary, that our Father in heaven may deliver us from all kinds of evil—affecting body or soul, property or reputation—and at last, when our final hour comes, may grant us a blessed end and take us by grace from this valley of tears to himself in heaven.

This petition includes all the evil that may befall us under the devil's kingdom: poverty, disgrace, death, and, in short, all the tragic misery and heartache, of which there is so incalculably much on earth… Therefore, there is nothing for us to do on earth but to pray without ceasing against this archenemy. For if God did not support us, we would not be safe from him for a single hour.

BIBLICAL WISDOM

For the one who is in you is greater than the one who is in the world. 1 John 4:4

SILENCE FOR MEDITATION

QUESTIONS TO PONDER

- If God in Christ is the victor, what should the Christian's attitude toward evil, or Satan, be?
- How should the Christian's attitude toward evil be translated into action?
- Although Luther saw a terrible conflict going on between Christ and the devil (evil), would he advise us to flee the world? Why or why not?

PSALM FRAGMENT

Hear my voice, O God, in my complaint;
preserve my life from the dread enemy. Psalm 64:1

Journal Reflections

- Reflect on your own experience, or a friend's, in which you felt oppressed or attacked by Satan or evil. What spiritual resources were you able to bring to the experience? What happened?
- Think about some problem you are facing. How might the knowledge that God is supporting you change the way you deal with this problem?
- Some people pray the last petition of the Lord's prayer, "Deliver us from the evil one." Would it make a difference in your praying the Lord's Prayer if you said it that way? Explain.

Prayers for the Life of Faith

Pray that you will have confidence in the power of God to hear your prayers and deliver you and those you love and care for from the power of the evil one.

Prayer for Today

Almighty and merciful God, deliver us from the evil one. Keep me always certain that you, through your Son Jesus Christ, can deliver me from his power, and give me the confidence that you will hear my prayers and keep me close.

Notes

AMEN.

What is this?

Answer: That I should be certain that such petitions are acceptable to and heard by our Father in heaven, for he himself commanded us to pray like this and has promised to hear us. "Amen, amen" means "Yes, yes, it is going to come about just like this."

The efficacy of prayer consists in our learning also to say AMEN to it—that is, not to doubt that our prayer is surely heard and will be answered. This word is nothing else than an unquestioning word of faith on the part of the one who does not pray as a matter of luck but knows that God does not lie because he has promised to grant it. Where there is not faith like this, there also can be no true prayer.

BIBLICAL WISDOM

Are any among you suffering? They should pray. Are any cheerful? They should sing songs of praise. Are any among you sick? They should call for the elders of the church and have them pray over them, anointing them with oil in the name of the Lord. The prayer of faith will save the sick, and the Lord will raise them up; and anyone who has committed sins will be forgiven. Therefore confess your sins to one another, and pray for one another, so that you may be healed. The prayer of the righteous is powerful and effective. James 5:13-16

SILENCE FOR MEDITATION

QUESTIONS TO PONDER

- What is the difference between praying "as a matter of luck" and praying as a matter of faith?
- Why is faith necessary for true prayer?
- Is God a liar if your prayer does not appear to come true? Why or why not?

PSALM FRAGMENT

But truly God has listened;
he has given heed to the words of my prayer.
Blessed be God,
because he has not rejected my prayer
or removed his steadfast love from me. Psalm 66:19-10

JOURNAL REFLECTIONS

- Meditate on the word "Amen." What do you understand by the word? What feelings does the saying of this word after prayer evoke for you?
- Journal about how you understand the "efficacy" of your prayers. Make a list of prayers that you know have been answered and note how they were answered. Be specific. Where they always answered in the way you hoped or expected?
- Remember a time when your prayer was answered in a way other than how you had hoped. Write about the experience. What did you learn?

PRAYERS FOR THE LIFE OF FAITH

Pray that you can say Amen to your own prayers, trusting and believing that God will grant your prayer.

PRAYER FOR TODAY

Dear Jesus, you are the Amen of my prayers. Help me to believe truly in your word and in the promise of God that our prayers will be answered.

NOTES

WHAT IS CONFESSION?

Answer: Confession consists of two parts. One is that we confess our sins. The other is that we receive the absolution, that is, forgiveness, from the confessor as from God himself and by no means doubt but firmly believe that our sins are thereby forgiven before God in heaven.

[As to Confession] I refer to the practice of confessing to God alone or to our neighbor alone, asking for forgiveness. These two kinds are included in the Lord's Prayer when we say, 'Forgive us our debts, as we forgive our debtors.' Indeed, the entire Lord's Prayer is nothing else than such a confession. For what is our prayer but a confession that we neither have nor do what we ought and a plea for grace and a joyful conscience? This kind of confession should and must take place continuously as long as we live. For this is the essence of a genuinely Christian life, to acknowledge that we are sinners and to pray for grace.

⌁

BIBLICAL WISDOM

This is the message we have heard from him and proclaim to you, that God is light and in him there is no darkness at all. If we say that we have fellowship with him while we are walking in darkness, we lie and do not do what is true; but if we walk in the light as he himself is in the light, we have fellowship with one another, and the blood of Jesus his Son cleanses us from all sin. If we say that we have no sin, we deceive ourselves, and the truth is not in us. If we confess our sins, he who is faithful and just will forgive us our sins and cleanse us from all unrighteousness. If we say that we have not sinned, we make him a liar, and his word is not in us. 1 John 1:5-10

SILENCE FOR MEDITATION

Questions to Ponder

- Why is confession the "essence of a genuinely Christian life"?
- Why do we need to be exhorted and encouraged to confess our sins either to another or to God alone? What is the role of the church?
- The reading from 1 John points to our ability to deceive ourselves when it comes to sin. How does our culture encourage such self-deception? How can we learn to avoid such self-deception?

Psalm Fragment

Then I acknowledged my sin to you,
*   and I did not hide my iniquity;*
I said, "I will confess my transgressions to the Lord,"
*   and you forgave the guilt of my sin.* Psalm 32:5

Journal Reflections

- Meditate on the word "confession." What feelings does it evoke in you? Do you resist the idea or embrace it as a positive spiritual practice? Why?
- Meditate on the Lord's Prayer and then journal about how this prayer can be used as a daily experience of confession and forgiveness.
- Meditate on what it means to "walk in the light." Have you ever experienced light breaking over your soul after an experience of confession and forgiveness? If so, describe the experience and what you learned from it.

Prayers for the Life of Faith

Pray that you will learn to live in daily confession and forgiveness so that you will be able to walk in the light with Christ.

Prayer for Today

Dear Heavenly Father, forgive me my sins as I forgive those who have sinned against me. Teach me to revel in your grace.

Notes

Journey

Day 39

WHAT SINS IS A PERSON to confess?

Before God one is to acknowledge the guilt for all sins, even those of which we are not aware, as we do in the Lord's prayer. However, before the confessor we are to confess only those sins of which we have knowledge and which trouble us.

We are to confess our guilt before one another and forgive one another before we come to God and ask for forgiveness. Now, all of us are debtors to one another; therefore we should and we may confess publicly in everyone's presence, no one being afraid of anyone else. For it is true, as the proverb says, "If one person is upright, so are they all"; no one behaves toward God or the neighbor as he or she ought. However, besides the sum total of our sin, there are also individual ones, when a person has provoked someone else to anger and needs to ask for pardon. Thus we have in the Lord's Prayer a twofold absolution: both our sins against God and against our neighbors are forgiven when we forgive our neighbors and become reconciled with them.

BIBLICAL WISDOM

So when you are offering your gift at the altar, if you remember that your brother or sister has something against you, leave your gift there before the altar and go; first be reconciled to your brother or sister, and then come and offer your gift.
Matthew 5:23-24

SILENCE FOR MEDITATION

QUESTIONS TO PONDER

- Do you think confession is about guilt and shame or about grace and freedom? Explain.
- Why does a relationship with God and our relationships with others need both confession and forgiveness in order to thrive?

- Does your community of faith place too little, enough, or too much emphasis on confession and forgiveness in both our relationship with God and in our human relationships? Explain.

PSALM FRAGMENT

Search me, O God, and know my heart;
*   test me and know my thoughts.*
See if there is any wicked way in me,
*   and lead me in the way everlasting.* Psalm 139:23-24

JOURNAL REFLECTIONS

- The *daily* practice of confession and forgiveness with both God and others can be seen as a regular practice that builds our relationship with God. If this is a spiritual habit you presently are following, write about its impact on your life. If you are not following this practice now, why not give it a try?
- Remember a time when you knew you needed to ask someone for pardon. What did you do? What were the consequences?
- Journal on a moment in your life when you experienced reconciliation with another through confession and forgiveness. What did you learn from the experience? Has the learning stayed with you as a guide?

PRAYERS FOR THE LIFE OF FAITH

Pray that you will be given the grace and courage to ask forgiveness whenever it is necessary and that the other would have the grace and courage to forgive you.

PRAYER FOR TODAY

Lord Jesus, I long for reconciliation with [name]. Lead me and guide me so that I have the grace both to ask for forgiveness and to forgive.

NOTES

Journey

Day 40

IT WAS NOT UNINTENDED TO God's particular ordering of things that a lowly Christian person who might be unable to read the Bible should nevertheless be obligated to learn and know the Ten Commandments, the Creed and the Lord's Prayer. Indeed, the total content of Scripture and preaching and everything a Christian needs to know is quite fully and adequately comprehended in these three items… Three things a person must know in order to be saved. First, he must know what to do and what to leave undone. Second, when he realized that he cannot measure up to what he should do or leave undone, he needs to know where to go to find the strength he requires. Third, he must know how to seek and obtain the strength.

BIBLICAL WISDOM

At that same hour Jesus rejoiced in the Holy Spirit and said, "I thank you, Father, Lord of heaven and earth, because you have hidden these things from the wise and the intelligent and have revealed them to infants; yes, Father, for such was your gracious will." Luke 10:21

SILENCE FOR MEDITATION

QUESTIONS TO PONDER

- Why do you suppose that the things necessary for salvation are so simple and easily understood? Where does a person go to learn these simple things?
- Jesus is thankful these things are revealed to the babes, not the wise and prudent. Why do you think that is?
- At the same time, these things are so deep even the brilliant Luther said he did not understand them. Why?

PSALM FRAGMENT

Praise the LORD!
Praise the name of the LORD;
give praise, O servants of the LORD,
you that stand in the house of the LORD,
in the courts of the house of our God.
Praise the LORD, for the LORD is good;
sing to his name, for he is gracious. Psalm 135:1-3

JOURNAL REFLECTIONS

• Write down the three things Luther says you have to know and reflect on how much more deeply you understand them now after these forty days.
• Luther saw knowing the Commandments, Creed, and Lord's Prayer as an obligation for all Christians. Do you agree with him? Why or why not?
• Have you made the Catechism part of your daily devotions? If you have, what difference has it made in your daily life?

PRAYERS FOR THE LIFE OF FAITH

Thank God for the time you have spent learning from Martin Luther about the life of the Christian, what you should know and how you should pray.

PRAYER FOR TODAY

Dear Heavenly Father, I am overflowing with thanksgiving to you, for revealing to me so much of yourself in your Son Jesus, through the work of the Holy Spirit. Thank you for your faithful servant Martin Luther and what he has taught me now.

NOTES

Journey's End

You have finished your *40-Day Journey with Martin Luther*. I hope it has been a good journey and that along the way you have learned much, experienced much, and found good resources to deepen your faith and practice. As a result of this journey:

- How are you different?
- What have you learned?
- What have you experienced?
- In what ways has your faith and practice been transformed?

Notes

Do you want to continue the journey? If you would, there is a list of books about and by Martin Luther on the next page that will help you delve further into the thought, experience, and practice of this remarkable man.

FOR FURTHER READING

Roland Bainton. *Here I Stand: A Life of Martin Luther.* Nashville: Abingdon, 1950, 1978.

James Kittelson. *Luther the Reformer: The Story of the Man and his Career.* Minneapolis: Augsburg, 1986.

Heiko Obermann, *Luther: Man between God and the Devil.* New Haven: Yale University Press, 1986.

WORKS BY MARTIN LUTHER

Luther: Letters of Spiritual Counsel. Theodore E. Tappert, ed. Louisville: Westminster John Knox, 2006.

Luther's Works—American Edition, 55 volumes. Philadelphia: Fortress Press; St. Louis: Concordia, 1955-86.

Selected Writings of Martin Luther. Theodore E. Tappert, ed. Minneapolis: Fortress Press, 2007.

"Small Catechism" and "Large Catechism." In Wengert and Kolb, eds. *The Book of Concord.* Minneapolis: Fortress Press, 2000.

NOTES

Page 9, paragraph 2: Martin Luther, *Large Catechism* in Wengert and Kolb, eds., *The Book of Concord* (Minneapolis: Fortress Press, 2000), 385.
Page 20, paragraph 1: James Kittelson, *Luther the Reformer: The Story of the Man and his Career* (Minneapolis: Augsburg, 1986), 216-17.

Sources

Day 1: *Luther's Works,* Vol. 43, 193

Day 2: *Luther's Works,* Vol. 43, 193-95

Day 3: *Luther's Works,* Vol. 43, 199-200

Day 4: *Luther's Works,* Vol. 43, 200-201

Day 5: *Book of Concord, Large Catechism,* 444

Day 6: *Book of Concord, Small Catechism,* 351; *Book of Concord, Large Catechism,* 386

Day 7: *Book of Concord, Small Catechism,* 352; *Book of Concord, Large Catechism,* 394

Day 8: *Book of Concord, Small Catechism,* 352; *Book of Concord, Large Catechism,* 398

Day 9: *Book of Concord, Small Catechism,* 352; *Book of Concord, Large Catechism,* 401

Day 10: *Book of Concord, Small Catechism,* 352; *Book of Concord, Large Catechism,* 412

Day 11: *Book of Concord, Small Catechism,* 353; *Book of Concord, Large Catechism,* 414

Day 12: *Book of Concord, Small Catechism,* 353; *Book of Concord, Large Catechism,* 419-20

Day 13: *Book of Concord, Small Catechism,* 353; *Book of Concord, Large Catechism,* 421

Day 14: *Book of Concord, Small Catechism,* 353-54; *Book of Concord, Large Catechism,* 427

Day 15: *Book of Concord, Large Catechism,* 429

Day 16: *Book of Concord, Large Catechism,* 431

Day 17: *Book of Concord, Large Catechism,* 431

Day 18: *Book of Concord, Large Catechism,* 432

Day 19: *Book of Concord, Small Catechism,* 354; *Book of Concord, Large Catechism,* 433

Day 20: *Book of Concord, Small Catechism,* 355; *Book of Concord, Large Catechism,* 434

Day 21: *Book of Concord, Small Catechism,* 355; *Book of Concord, Large Catechism,* 434-35

Day 22: *Book of Concord, Small Catechism,* 355; *Book of Concord, Large Catechism,* 435-36

Day 23: *Book of Concord, Small Catechism,* 355-56; *Book of Concord, Large Catechism,* 438

Day 24: *Book of Concord, Large Catechism,* 441

Day 25: *Book of Concord, Large Catechism,* 443

Day 26: *Book of Concord, Small Catechism,* 357; *Book of Concord, Large Catechism,* 445

Day 27: *Book of Concord, Small Catechism,* 356; *Book of Concord, Large Catechism,* 446

Day 28: *Book of Concord, Small Catechism,* 356; *Book of Concord, Large Catechism,* 446-47

Day 29: *Book of Concord, Small Catechism,* 356-57; *Book of Concord, Large Catechism,* 447

Day 30: *Book of Concord, Small Catechism,* 357; *Book of Concord, Large Catechism,* 448

Day 31: *Book of Concord, Small Catechism,* 357; *Book of Concord, Large Catechism,* 449

Day 32: *Book of Concord, Small Catechism,* 357; *Book of Concord, Large Catechism,* 449-50

Day 33: *Book of Concord, Small Catechism,* 357; *Book of Concord, Large Catechism,* 451

Day 34: *Book of Concord, Small Catechism,* 358; *Book of Concord, Large Catechism,* 453

Day 35: *Book of Concord, Small Catechism,* 358; *Book of Concord, Large Catechism,* 454

Day 36: *Book of Concord, Small Catechism,* 358; *Book of Concord, Large Catechism,* 455-56

Day 37: *Book of Concord, Small Catechism,* 358; *Book of Concord, Large Catechism,* 456

Day 38: *Book of Concord, Small Catechism,* 360; *Book of Concord, Large Catechism,* 477

Day 39: *Book of Concord, Small Catechism,* 360; *Book of Concord, Large Catechism,* 477

Day 40: *Luther's Works,* Vol. 43, 13

We gratefully acknowledge the publishers who granted permission to reprint material from the following sources:

Excerpts from *The Book of Concord,* ed. Robert Kolb and Timothy J. Wengert, are copyright © 2000 Augsburg Fortress.

Excerpts from *Luther's Works, Vol. 43: Devotional Writings II,* ed. Gustav K. Wiencke are copyright © 1959 Fortress Press, admin. Augsburg Fortress.

James Kittelson, *Luther the Reformer: The Story of the Man and his Career.* Augsburg Publishing House, Minneapolis, 1986, 216-17.

NOTES

NOTES

NOTES

CPSIA information can be obtained
at www.ICGtesting.com
Printed in the USA
FFOW03n0618031216

2996 4FF